Excel for Auditors

by Bill Jelen and Dwayne K. Dowell

Holy Macro! Books

Excel for Auditors
© 2007 Tickling Keys

Written by:
Bill Jelen and Dwayne K. Dowell

Edited by:
Linda DeLonais

On the Cover:
Design by Shannon Mattiza, 6'4 Productions.

Published by:
Holy Macro! Books
PO Box 82
Uniontown, Ohio, USA 44685

Distributed by:
Independent Publishers Group

First printing:
September 2006.
Printed in the United States of America

Library of Congress Data
Excel for Auditors /Bill Jelen and Dwayne K. Dowell
Library of Congress Control Number: 2006931383

ISBN: 1-932802-16-9

Table of Contents

About the Authors

Bill Jelen

Bill Jelen is the host of MrExcel.com. You can catch him at one of his Power Excel Seminars around the country or on his daily two-minute video podcast. He is the author of twelve books about Microsoft Excel, including Pivot Table Data Crunching and Guerilla Data Analysis Using Microsoft Excel. He has made over 50 guest appearances on TV's Call for Help with Leo Laporte.

Before founding MrExcel.com in 1998, Jelen spent twelve years "in the trenches", as a financial analyst for the accounting, finance, marketing, and operations departments of a publicly held company. Since then, his company automates Excel reports for hundreds of clients around the world

Dwayne K. Dowell

Dwayne K. Dowell is the founder of Dwayne K. Dowell, PSC, a CPA firm located in Louisville, KY. In addition to be a Certified Public Accountant, Dwayne is a Certified Fraud Examiner and Certified Internal Auditor. His work history includes over 21 years of experience, with fourteen years in public accounting and over seven years in private industry as a Chief Financial Officer in the health care industry.

He is a member of the American Institute of Certified Public Accountants, the Association of Certified Fraud Examiners, the Institute of Internal Auditors, the Institute of Managerial Accountants, and the Association of Certified Anti-Money Laundering Specialists

Copying a Worksheet

READ THIS!

You may think you know how to copy a worksheet – but I'll bet that you don't. I guarantee this one will save you anywhere from five to 30 minutes, depending on the size of your worksheet (and how compulsive you are about your settings).

Here's the Situation

A worksheet contains more than data and formulas. There is page setup data; there are column widths, etc. When you copy cells from one worksheet to a new worksheet, you will copy the cell contents, but not the meta data (configuration information) about the sheet. There are several variations on the Move or Copy Sheet command.

Here's What to Do

1. If you need to make a copy of a worksheet and place it in the same workbook, simply hold down the Ctrl key while you drag the sheet to a new location.

> **Figure 1**   Plus sign above cursor indicates that you are copying the worksheet

Copying a Worksheet

2. The new worksheet is given a strange name such as Jan(2), Jan(3), etc. Double-click the sheet tab to rename the sheet.

Figure 2   Changing the default name of a copied worksheet

3. To access the full range of options for the Move or Copy command, right-click the worksheet tab and choose "Move or Copy".

Figure 3

Selecting "Move or Copy" from the right-click menu

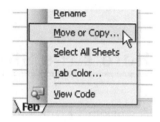

In the default settings for the Move or Copy dialog, Excel will move the worksheet to a new location in the current workbook. This is somewhat unnecessary, since you can easily move a worksheet by simply dragging the tab to a new location.

Figure 4

Using Move or Copy dialog box to move a different worksheet to a new location in the same or in another workbook and to make a copy of that worksheet

 Tip:

Click and drag a worksheet tab to move the worksheet to a new area in the same workbook.

4. Choose the box for "Create a copy" to have Excel make an exact copy of the worksheet.

5. Finally, use the dropdown at the top.
    If you want to make a copy of a worksheet in a new workbook or copy it to another open workbook, you can choose this in the "To book" dropdown.

Copying a
Worksheet

Figure 5

Moving a worksheet to a new workbook

Excel Details

Using this command offers many advantages over copying and pasting cells. Excel will copy:

- Column widths and row heights

- Cell formatting

- Print Setup information such as headers and footers

- View Manager and Scenario Manager settings

**Copying a
Worksheet**

Showing Numbers in Thousands

Here's the Situation

If you are analyzing sales for a $100 Million company, it does not make sense to show sales to the penny or dollar.

	A	B
1	**Customer**	**Total**
2	Wal-Mart	869454.17
3	Verizon	390978.85
4	Texaco	34364.91
5	Sun Life Financial	498937.48
6	State Farm	59881.62
7	Shell Canada	71651.70

Figure 6

Sales data for large amounts should not show cents

How can you display results in thousands or millions?

Here's What to Do

There are custom number formats to display results in thousands, but they are not found on the Formatting toolbar.

1. Select the range of cells containing the numeric data. Press Ctrl+1 (that is, Ctrl plus the number 1) to display the Format Cells dialog.

 Tip:

When you want to set up a custom format, it is best to choose a standard numeric format to get close. Use either the numeric or currency category and change the decimal places to zero.

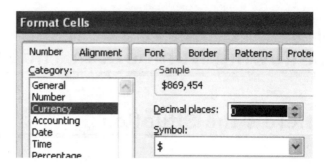

Figure 7

Changing number of decimal places to zero

Showing #s
in 1000s

2. Choose Custom from the bottom of the Category list.

Notice that you are starting with a custom number format of "$#,##0". This is the format that Excel built for you to display currency with zero decimal places.

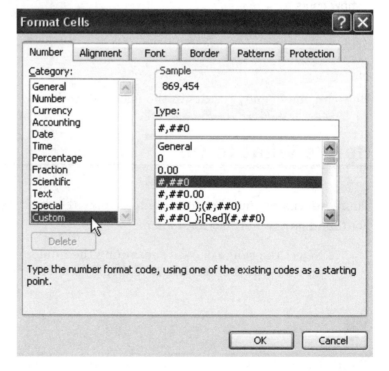

Figure 8

Selecting a custom number format from the Type dropdown

Tip:

If you place a comma at the end of this custom number format, Excel will keep the original number, but divide it by one thousand when it displays it in the cell. In the Sample box below, you will see that $869,454 is now displayed as $869.

3. Add a comma at the end of the custom number format.

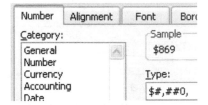

Figure 9

Changing the custom format to divide the original number by one thousand

Gotcha

To make it clear that the numbers are in thousands, you could note this in the title of your report. Or, you can add an abbreviation to the custom number format. If your company uses "K" as the abbreviation for one thousand, then a custom number format of $#,##0,K is valid. However, to use "M" for the thousands abbreviation, you will have to put the M in quotes: $#,##0,"M"

Figure 10

Using "M" for the thousands abbreviation

Excel Details

Every comma at the end of the custom number format will cause the displayed number to be divided by another thousand. Thus, to display numbers in millions, put two commas at the end of the format. To display numbers rounded to the nearest hundred thousand, it is valid to combine a decimal place followed by two commas. The following table shows the effect of various custom formats on the same number.

Table 1

Using custom formats to change the way a number displays

Custom Format	Result
0.00	1234567.89
0	1234568
#,##0	1,234,568
#,##0,K	1,235K
#,##0.0,,"M"	1.2M
$#,##0,,"M"	$1M
$#,##0.0,,"M"	$1.2M

M for thousands, MM for millions

#,##0,"M"	1,235M
$#,##0,,"MM"	$1MM

Quickly Seeing Sum or Average

Here's the Situation

Your CFO calls you on the phone and starts asking you questions. He asks questions like "How much did Shell Canada buy last year?", "What was the largest order from Nortel?", and "What was the average order from Kroger?".

Here's What to Do

You can answer these questions quickly without creating any formulas in Excel. In fact, if you can click the mouse quietly, your CFO might actually believe that you *do* know this stuff off the top of your head!

1. Select a single cell in the Customer column and click the AZ button in the Standard toolbar to sort the data by Customer.

 Caution!

Be sure to select just a single cell. Selecting more than one will sort just the selected cells, which can really mess up your data. If this happens, press the Undo button or Ctrl+Z *before* you do anything else!

2. Scroll until you find the section of records for Shell Canada. Highlight the cells that contain revenue for those records.

Seeing Sum/Avg

Figure 11

Selecting the range of cells you want to sum

	D	E	F
1	**Customer**	**Quantity**	**Revenue**
407	Sears	600	12612
408	Sears Canada	800	16784
409	Sears Canada	300	5532
410	Sears Canada	800	18264
411	Sears Canada	800	16936
412	Shell Canada	1000	20950
413	Shell Canada	500	9635
414	Shell Canada	800	16936
415	Shell Canada	1000	24130
416	State Farm	200	4754

 Note:

Some installations of Excel have the Status Bar turned off. You might have to use View – Status Bar to turn the Status Bar back on.

3. Now – look in the Status Bar at the bottom of the screen.
   The Status Bar generally says "Ready" on the left side. In the right half of the status bar, you will see the words "Sum=71651". This represents the sum of the selected cells. So – the answer to the boss' first question is that Shell Canada purchased $71,651 from the company last year.

Figure 12

Sum of the selected block of cells

Sum=71651   NUM

4. Scroll up and highlight the revenue for Nortel.
   In this case, there are 28 cells in the selection. The status bar reveals that Nortel purchased $406K last year, but your boss wants to know the largest order from Nortel.

5. Right click on the Sum field and choose Max.

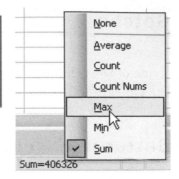

Figure 13

Selecting Max from the Sum field's right-click menu (Take note of the other options available in the right-click menu)

Seeing Sum/Avg

Sum=406326

The status bar reveals that the largest order from Nortel was $25,350.

Figure 14   Finding the maximum value in a range of cells

Max=25350

6. Next the boss wants to know the average order from Kroger. Highlight the cells for Kroger revenue. Right-click the status bar figure and choose Average.

Figure 15

Finding the average value in a range of cells

307	IBM	100	2213	1022	1191	5:
308	Kroger	800	19520	7872	11648	5!
309	Kroger	100	1819	847	972	5:
310	Kroger	100	2538	1022	1516	5!
311	Kroger	1000	22840	10220		None
312	Lucent	300	7167	3066		Average
313	Lucent	700	14497	6888		
314	Lucent	1000	17190	8470		Count
315	Lucent	1000	23890	10220		Count Nums
316	Molson, Inc	600	10602	5082		Max
317	Molson, Inc	100	1817	847		Min

Pivot Table

Sum

Average=11679.25

Gotcha

If one of the cells in your selection contains an error such as #VALUE! or #NA!, the QuickSum feature will turn off.

Better in Excel 2007

The Status Bar in Excel 2007 can show several values at once.

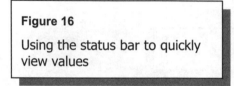

Figure 16

Using the status bar to quickly view values

411	Sears Canada	800	16936	8176
412	Shell Canada	1000	20950	9840
413	Shell Canada	500	9635	4235
414	Shell Canada	800	16936	8176
415	Shell Canada	1000	24130	10220
416	State Farm	200	4754	1968

Pivot Table

Average: 17912.75   Count: 4   Sum: 71651

To customize the Status Bar in Excel 2007, right-click it to display the configuration menu. You can control which items are, or are not, visible.

Figure 17

Selecting items visible in, and configuring, the Status Bar in Excel 2007

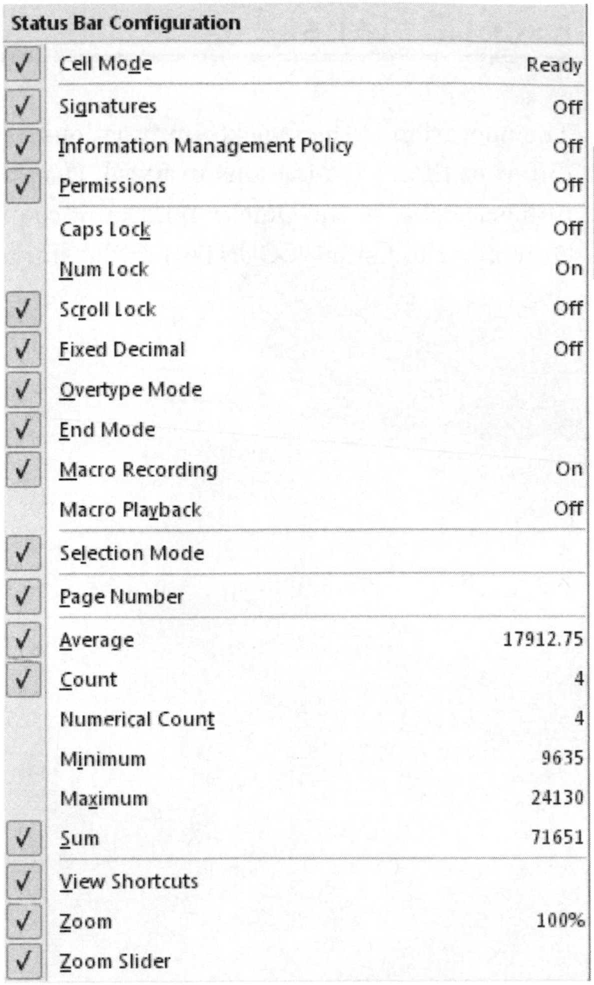

Status Bar Configuration		
✓	Cell Mode	Ready
✓	Signatures	Off
✓	Information Management Policy	Off
✓	Permissions	Off
	Caps Lock	Off
	Num Lock	On
✓	Scroll Lock	Off
✓	Fixed Decimal	Off
✓	Overtype Mode	
✓	End Mode	
✓	Macro Recording	On
	Macro Playback	Off
✓	Selection Mode	
✓	Page Number	
✓	Average	17912.75
✓	Count	4
	Numerical Count	4
	Minimum	9635
	Maximum	24130
✓	Sum	71651
✓	View Shortcuts	
✓	Zoom	100%
✓	Zoom Slider	

Excel Details

Seeing Sum/Avg

The operation of the QuickSum functions for Count and CountNums is different than the functions in Excel. Usually, the COUNT function counts only numeric cells. In the QuickSum, Count counts all non-blank cells. This is equivalent to using =COUNTA() in the spreadsheet.

Adding Subtotals

Here's the Situation

You have sales data for three dozen of your best customers. You would like to
see totals by customer. You might be tempted to insert blank rows between
each customer and use the AutoSum button to add totals. This might work for
a few customers, but it would take too long for a large number of customers.

Figure 18

Chart of sales data for top three dozen customers

	A	B	C	D	E	F	G	H
1	**Region**	**Product**	**Date**	**Customer**	**Quantity**	**Revenue**	**COGS**	**Profit**
10	West	ABC	16-Sep-04	Ainsworth	100	1741	847	894
11	East	ABC	4-Nov-04	Ainsworth	400	8468	3388	5080
12	Central	DEF	9-Dec-04	Ainsworth	600	12888	5904	6984
13	West	ABC	31-Mar-04	Air Canada	300	5859	2541	3318
14	Central	XYZ	19-Apr-04	Air Canada	200	4948	2044	2904
15	West	XYZ	24-Aug-04	Air Canada	800	17856	8176	9680
16	East	DEF	7-Oct-04	Air Canada	100	2358	984	1374
17	East	DEF	13-Apr-04	Bell Canada	600	14004	5904	8100
18	Central	DEF	24-Jun-04	Bell Canada	200	4060	1968	2092
19	West	XYZ	31-Aug-04	Bell Canada	800	18072	8176	9896
20	West	ABC	4-Nov-04	Bell Canada	800	15104	6776	8328
21	Central	DEF	26-Feb-04	Chevron	900	20610	8856	11754
22	East	ABC	15-Mar-04	Chevron	400	8116	3388	4728

Here's What to Do

Instead, use automatic subtotals.

1. Select a single cell in the customer column. Press AZ in the Standard toolbar to ensure that your data is sorted by Customer. In Excel 97-2003, from the Data menu, select Subtotals. In Excel 2007, select Subtotal from the Outline group of the Data ribbon.

Note:

The Subtotals command is excellent, but it has some quirky defaults. Excel always assumes that you want to subtotal by the left-most column in your dataset. It also assumes that you want to apply the subtotals to the right-most column in your dataset. If that column contains text, then the Subtotals dialog will change the Function selection from Sum to Count.

Figure 19 Changing the field, function, and target location for subtotals

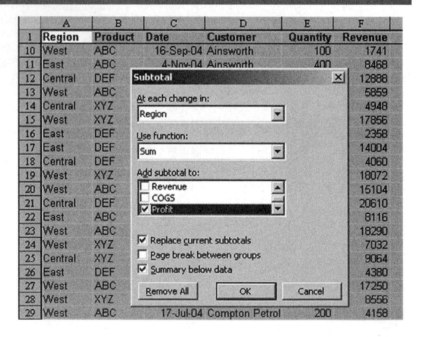

In the current case, you want to subtotal each Customer.

 Tips:

If you have more than three columns to subtotal, you need to scroll up to select other fields.

If you need each customer to print on a separate page, select the "Page break between groups" option.

2. Change the top dropdown from Region to Customer.

    In this case, the function of Sum is correct.

    In the Subtotal list, keep Profit checked and check COGS and Revenue.

Figure 20

Changing Subtotal dialog choices

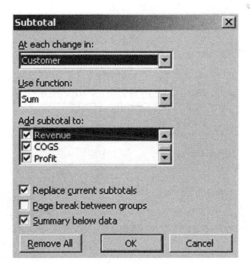

3. When you click OK, Excel automatically inserts a new row between each customer. The Subtotals command will insert a special function called Subtotal. The Subtotal function will sum rows in the range, but it is smart enough to ignore other subtotals in the range.

Figure 21

Subtotal buttons
let you determine
the subtotal level
to display

F13		▼	fx	=SUBTOTAL(9,F2:F12)	
1 2 3		C	D	E	F	G
	1	Date	Customer	Quantity	Revenue	COGS
	10	16-Sep-04	Ainsworth	100	1741	847
	11	4-Nov-04	Ainsworth	400	8468	3388
	12	9-Dec-04	Ainsworth	600	12888	5904
	13		**Ainsworth Total**		110367	48643
	14	31-Mar-04	Air Canada	300	5859	2541
	15	19-Apr-04	Air Canada	200	4948	2044

Notice that Excel has added three small buttons (1, 2, and 3) to the left of the
row numbers. If you press the 2 button, Excel will show you only the subtotal
rows.

 Tips:

Pressing button 2 is a great way to print a summary report.

Pressing button 1 shows you only the grand totals.

Pressing button 3 shows all of the rows.

Figure 22

Pressing button 2
displays only the
subtotals

D	E	F	G	H
Customer	Quantity	Revenue	COGS	Profit
Ainsworth Total		110367	48643	61724
Air Canada Total		31021	13745	17276
Bell Canada Total		51240	22824	28416
Chevron Total		54048	23780	30268
Compaq Total		39250	18614	20636
Compton Petroleum Tota		31369	13730	17639
Exxon Total		704359	311381	392978
Ford Total		622794	274978	347816
General Motors Total		750163	334614	415549

Since the report shows only the subtotals, it would be cool if you could copy just
those subtotals to a new workbook. However, if you select the cells, copy, and
then paste, you will see that all of the hidden detail rows were copied as well.
Instead, use this method.

1.   Select the cells from the Grand Total to the header row.

2. In Excel 97-2003: From the menu, select Edit → Go To. On the Go To dialog, choose the Special button.

   In Excel 2007: Use Home → Editing → Find & Select → Go To Special.

Figure 23

Selecting the Special button on the Go To dialog

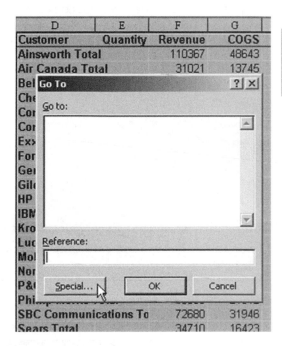

Adding Subtotals

3. On the Go To Special dialog, choose Visible Cells Only and press OK.

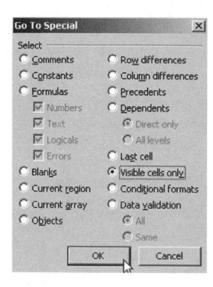

Figure 24

Selecting the "Visible cells only" option lets you copy and paste only the data you have displayed; hidden rows are not copied

The result will be that Excel selects just the visible rows. There are thin white bands in the data to indicate that the hidden rows are not selected.

Figure 25

Hidden rows are indicated by thin white bands

D	E	F
Customer	Quantity	Revenue
Ainsworth Total		110367
Air Canada Total		31021
Bell Canada Total		51240

You can now copy and paste to a new worksheet to get just the subtotal rows.

 Tip:

The awesome shortcut for Edit – Go To – Special – Visible Cells only is Alt+; (in other words, hold down Alt while pressing a semi-colon).

Excel Details

Removing Subtotals

To remove subtotals, choose Data → Subtotals again and select the Remove All button.

Adding Subtotals

Adding a Second Level of Subtotals

1. You can add a second level of subtotals. Sort the data by Product within Region.

2. Add subtotals to the Region field; then, select Data → Subtotals again.

3. This time, select Product and uncheck the option for "Replace Current Subtotals".

Figure 26

Adding a second level of subtotals allows you to see a summary based on two fields

The result will be a report with four Group & Outline buttons. Pressing button 3 will provide a summary by Region and Product.

Figure 27

Pressing button 3 provides a summary by Region and Product

1 2 3 4		A	B	C	D	E	F
	1	Region	Product	Date	Customer	Quantity	Revenue
+	69		ABC Total				694672
+	127		DEF Total				744348
+	191		XYZ Total				779958
−	192	Central Total					2218978
+	258		ABC Total				650063
+	328		DEF Total				800821
+	387		XYZ Total				831495
−	388	East Total					2282379
+	444		ABC Total				601411
+	484		DEF Total				459652
+	534		XYZ Total				686908
−	535	West Total					1747971
−	536	Grand Total					6249328

Quickly Filling a Series

Here's the Situation

If you have to fill a range with date data, there is often a way to do this quickly using the *Fill Handle*. When you select a cell or a range of cells, the fill handle is the square dot in the lower right corner of the selection.

Here's What to Do

1. Enter today's date in cell A1. Move the cell pointer back to A1.

 Tip:

Use Ctrl+; to enter today's date.

Figure 28

Drag a fill handle to fill a range with data

	A
1	12/2/2005
2	
3	

2. Grab the fill handle and drag down the column. As you drag, a tooltip will show you the date of the last cell in the range.

In the image below, the series would extend through December 12.

Figure 29

Tooltip shows the projected date of the selected range

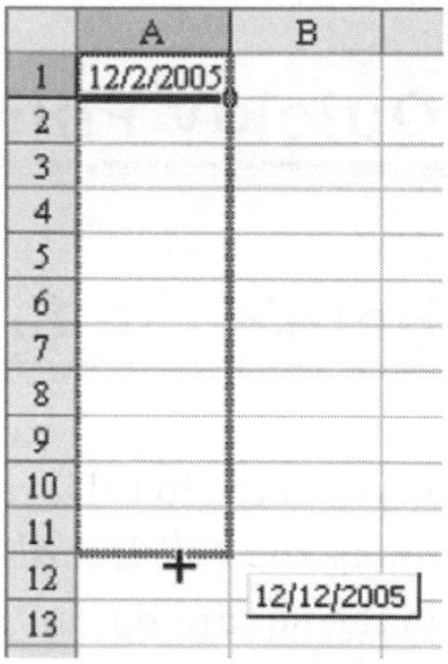

Filling a Series

3. Release the mouse button.

Excel extends the series, adding dates.

Figure 30

Excel fills in the range when the fill handle is released

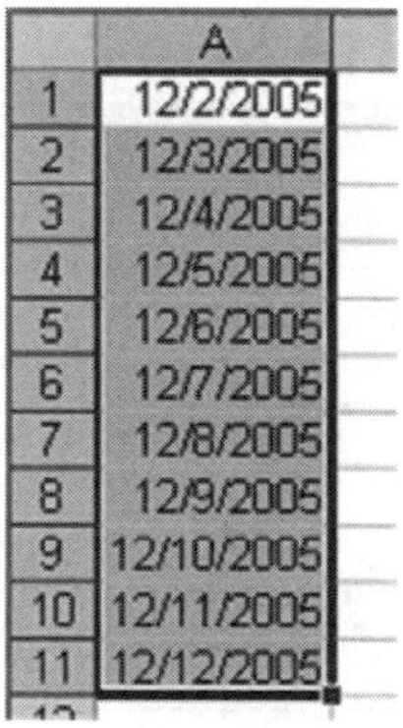

This trick works with many types of data.

4. Enter Jan in B1. Drag the fill handle and Excel fills in the months.

Figure 31

Using the fill handle to fill a range with month abbreviations

5. Enter Wednesday in C1 and drag the fill handle.

Figure 32

Using the fill handle to fill a range with dates

6.   Enter 1st Period in D1 and drag.

Figure 33

Using the fill handle to fill a range with numbered periods

7.   Enter 1 in E1 and drag.

Figure 34

Excel fails to fill in a range with consecutive numbers

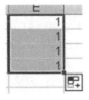

Wait! What's going on? Excel was able to extend all of the series for dates, months, days, periods, quarters, etc., but Excel can't figure out that this series should be 1, 2, 3?

8.   To extend this series, you will have to enter a "1" in E1 and a "2" in E2. Select both of those cells before you drag the fill handle.

| Figure 35 | Excel requires enough entries to define a unique series |

**Filling
a Series**

This process even allows you to fill a range with odd cells.

9. Enter a "1" in the first cell and a "3" in the second cell. Now drag the fill handle.

Figure 36

Filling a range with consecutive odd numbers

 Tip:

To extend a numeric series without entering two cells, enter a 1 in a cell. Ctrl+drag the fill handle to automatically extend the series to 1, 2, 3, etc. Similarly, if you Ctrl+drag a date, the date value will stay the same.

If you set up a custom list to control sort order (as described on page 72), you can type the first value and drag to extend that list.

1. My favorite trick is filling only weekdays. Enter a date in H1.

2. Use Ctrl+1 to format cells and select a format that shows the day of the week. With the cell pointer in H1, right-click the fill handle and drag.

3. The tooltip will make you believe that this is a normal fill, but when you release the right mouse button, a menu pops up. Select "Fill Weekdays" from the menu.

Figure 37

Selecting "Fill Weekdays" from the fill handle's right-click drop down menu

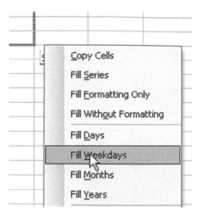

Filling
a Series

Excel fills the range with weekdays, skipping Saturdays and Sundays.

Figure 38

Filling range with weekdays

H
Friday, December 02, 2005
Monday, December 05, 2005
Tuesday, December 06, 2005
Wednesday, December 07, 2005
Thursday, December 08, 2005
Friday, December 09, 2005
Monday, December 12, 2005
Tuesday, December 13, 2005

**Filling
a Series**

Using a Fixed Value in Your Formula

Doesn't it just figure that Excel's most amazing built-in function can also cause quite a bit of frustration and error? I'm talking *Relative* and *Absolute References*. In English, this would be Excel's secret shorthand code to make sure that a copied formula always points to a particular cell or range.

Fixed Value in Formula

Here's the Situation

The worksheet below shows a variety of actual sales figures for several models.

Figure 39
Worksheet showing sales figures

	A	B	C	D
1	Forecasted Sales			
2				
3	Model	2005	2006	2007
4	Model 110	1,774K		
5	Model 120	1,176K		
6	Model 130	1,036K		
7	Model 140	987K		
8	Model 150	916K		
9	Model 160	1,406K		
10	Model 170	1,834K		
11	Model 180	1,932K		

1. To calculate forecasted sales, enter the formula =B4*1.05 in cell C4 and copy it to all of the other cells.

Figure 40

Calculating forecasted sales by copying the same formula to a range of cells using a relative reference and a fixed multiplicand

			D5		▼		*fx*	=C5*1.05		

	A	B	C	D	E	F	G
1	Forecasted Sales						
2							
3	Model	2005	2006	2007	2008	2009	2010
4	Model 110	1,774K	1,863K	1,956K	2,054K	2,156K	2,264K
5	Model 120	1,176K	1,235K	1,296K	1,361K	1,429K	1,501K
6	Model 130	1,036K	1,088K	1,142K	1,199K	1,259K	1,322K
7	Model 140	987K	1,036K	1,088K	1,142K	1,199K	1,259K
8	Model 150	916K	961K	1,009K	1,060K	1,113K	1,169K

You probably take it for granted, but it is slightly amazing that Excel converts the reference to "B4" in cell C4 to be "C5" when this formula is copied to cell D5.

2. Now, instead of entering 1.05 in the formula, enter 1.05 in cell D1 (D1 is formatted to display as a percentage) and have the formula in cell C4 point to =D1*1.05. This formula calculates the same result.

Figure 41

Calculating forecasted sales in a single cell using a formula with two relative references

	A	B	C	D	
1	Forecasted Sales			105%	
2					
3	Model	2005	2006	2007	20
4	Model 110	1,774K	1,863K		
5	Model 120	1,176K			

3. However, when you copy this formula to the other cells, something goes wrong. All of the forecasts are zero!.

Figure 42

Copying preceding formula to a range of cells produces unexpected results

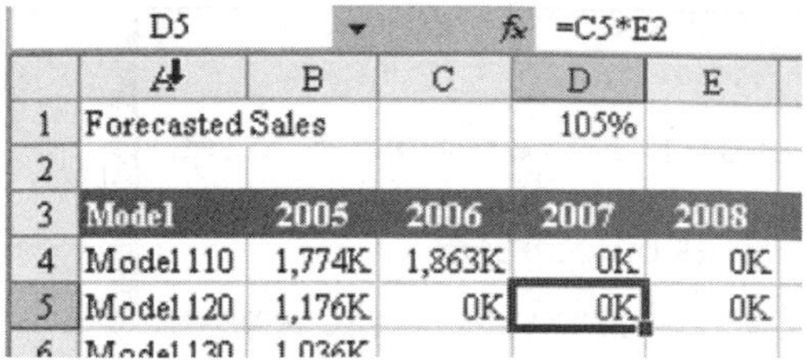

D5 =C5*E2

	A	B	C	D	E
1	Forecasted Sales			105%	
2					
3	Model	2005	2006	2007	2008
4	Model 110	1,774K	1,863K	0K	0K
5	Model 120	1,176K	0K	0K	0K
6	Model 130	1,036K			

When you copy the formula from C4 to D5, the reference pointing to B4 accurately changes to point to cell C5. This is what you want to happen. However, the reference that pointed to D1 also changed. It is now pointing to E2. Since cell E2 does not contain a growth rate, the result is zero.

How can you write a formula that will always multiply by D1?

Here's What to Do

References such as D1 and B4 are called *Relative References*. As you copy a formula containing relative references, the cell being referenced in the formula changes.

Sometimes, you want a cell reference to always point to a certain cell. In this case, you always want to use the growth rate in cell D1. To do this, change the reference style to an absolute reference by placing a dollar sign before the column letter and row number.

In this case, you need to change the formula in C4 to =B4*$D$1.

Now, as you copy the formula, the reference to B4 is allowed to change but every cell continues to point to the growth rate in D1. You can enter new growth rates in D1 to play what-if games.

Figure 43

Using relative references to see results of different forecasted sales percentages

	D5		▼	f_x =C5*$D$1	
	A	B	C	D	E
1	Forecasted Sales			107%	
2					
3	Model	2005	2006	2007	2008
4	Model 110	1,774K	1,898K	2,031K	2,173K
5	Model 120	1,176K	1,258K	1,346K	1,440K
6	Model 130	1,036K	1,108K	1,186K	1,269K

Fixed Value in Formula

Note that there are times where you want to freeze the row number but allow the column letter to move. In this case, a reference such as =C$1 will achieve that result. This is called a *Mixed Reference*.

Other times, you will want a formula to always refer to a value in column A, but it is OK to have the row number change. In this case, a reference such as =$A4 will work. This is also a mixed reference.

Excel Details

To simplify the entry of dollar signs in references, you can use the F4 key. When you are typing a formula, hit the F4 key immediately after typing a cell reference. The first time that you hit F4, the reference changes from =D1 to =$D$1. Hit F4 again to toggle to =D$1. Hit F4 again to toggle to =$D1. Hit F4 once more to toggle back to a relative reference of =D1.

Table 2

Table showing cycle pattern of reference states

Pressing F4	Result	Reference Status
Initial state	=D1	Relative
Press F4 once	=$D$1	Absolute
Press F4 twice	=D$1	Mixed (fixed column)
Press F4 three times	=$D1	Mixed (fixed row)
Press F4 four times	=D1	Relative

Replacing a Thousand Formulas with One

Here's the Situation

You have data that has 5000 records with quantity and unit price. You would like to calculate the sum of quantity times the unit price for all rows.

Figure 44

Dataset with 5000 records in which you need to find the sum of the quantity times the price for all rows

	A	B	C	D
1	Invoice	Item	Qty	Unit Price
2	1001	B83	30	$8.30
3	1001	A48	4	$4.80
4	1001	M72	29	$7.20
5	1001	B27	19	$2.70
6	1001	M99	28	$9.90
7	1001	D13	4	$1.30
8	1001	J83	38	$8.30
9	1001	T26	25	$2.60

Here's What to Do

Normally, you would enter =C2*D2 in E2, copy this formula down, and add a SUM formula.

Figure 45

Ordinary SUM formula

E5000			▼	f_x =D5000*C5000	
	A	B	C	D	E
1	Invoice	Item	Qty	Unit Price	
4996	1510	E21	15	$2.10	$31.50
4997	1510	T92	46	$9.20	$423.20
4998	1510	S28	5	$2.80	$14.00
4999	1510	L11	21	$1.10	$23.10
5000	1510	Z87	33	$8.70	$287.10
5001					$706,746.00

However, there is a secret kind of formula in Excel called an *Array Formula* or *CSE Formula*.

1. In cell D5001, enter =SUM(C2:C5000*D2:D5000).
    At first glance, this looks like an invalid formula. However, you are going to turn it into an array formula.

Figure 46

Using Ctrl+Shift+Enter to enter an array formula, which is indicated by the curly braces

21	15	$2.10	
T92	46	$9.20	
528	5	$2.80	
L11	21	$1.10	
Z87	33	$8.70	
		=sum(C2:C5000*D2:D5000)	

2. Press Ctrl+Shift+Enter. Excel adds curly braces around the formula and actually does the 5000 multiplications before showing you the result.

Figure 47

Using an array formula to sum the quantity times the unit price for all 5000 rows

D5001	▼		f_x {=SUM(C2:C5000*D2:D5000)}			
	A	B	C	D	E	F	G
1	Invoice	Item	Qty	Unit Price			
4998	1510	S28	5	$2.80			
4999	1510	L11	21	$1.10			
5000	1510	Z87	33	$8.70			
5001				$706,746.00			
5002							

Array formulas can occasionally come in very handy. I find it hard to remember the keystroke combination of Ctrl+Shift+Enter, so I call these CSE formulas to help me remember that I need to hold down **C**trl+**S**hift+**E**nter.

Excel Details

A few of these formulas work fine. However, if you try to build a report with thousands of array formulas, each evaluating thousands of cells, the recalculation time can become incredibly long.

Highlighting Outliers

Here's the Situation

You have a large dataset. You want to find the transactions which are out of the ordinary. Perhaps you want to find the largest or smallest transactions, or transactions above average.

Here's What to Do

Use the new *Conditional Formatting* options in Excel 2007.

The opportunities for highlighting outliers with conditional formatting have dramatically improved in Excel 2007. The combination of easy conditional formatting with the Sort by Color option is fantastic.

Most of the chapters in this book focus on illustrating how to do something in Excel 97-2003 and on how this is different in Excel 2007. However, the first 90% of this chapter focuses on the improved features in Excel 2007. The final example covers conditional formatting in Excel 2003.

Using Conditional Formatting in Excel 2007

To find the largest values in a range, select the range of numeric data.

1. On the Home ribbon, choose the Conditional Formatting dropdown arrow.

2. Click on the Top/Bottom Rules to open the flyout menu as shown in Figure 48.

Figure 48

The 2007 flyout menu offers far more and easier rules than Excel 2003

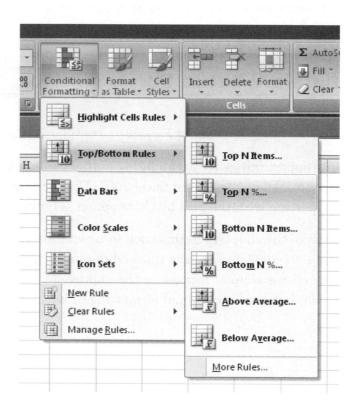

As shown in Figure 49, the next dialog box allows you to choose a particular percentage (%) value and a color scheme.

3. If you don't like one of the built in color schemes, choose Custom Format... and build your own scheme.

Figure 49

You can easily format cells in the top or bottom n%

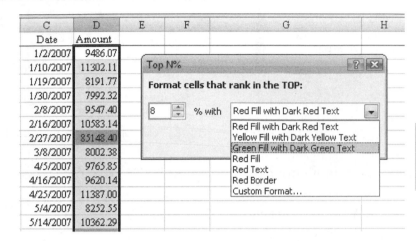

Finding Transactions from the Last Week

When your column contains dates, the conditional formatting in Excel 2007 can easily find dates that fit in a certain range.

1. Select a range of dates.

2. On the Home ribbon, click the Conditional Formatting dropdown.

3. Click on Highlight Cells Rules.

4. Click on A Date Occurring..., as shown in Figure 50.

Figure 50

Conditional formatting can highlight cells based on values, text, dates or duplicates

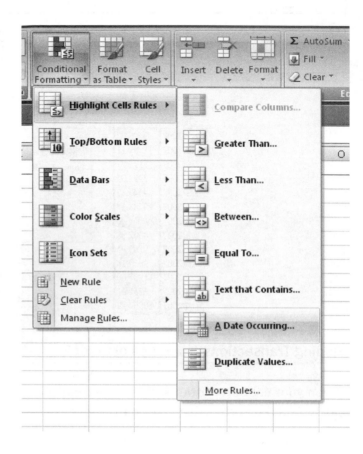

As shown in Figure 51, you can use the dropdown in the A Date Occurring dialog to ask for dates that occur in certain time periods, such as yesterday, this week, or next month. These ranges are re-evaluated every time you open the workbook. If you set up rules to highlight the items due "Today", you will see different items highlighted, depending on the date in the system clock.

Figure 51

Select a logical date range from the dropdown

Using Icon Sets to Mark Values

Icon Sets are a new feature in Excel 2007.

1. Select a range of values. From the Home ribbon, choose Conditional Formatting → Icon Sets → More Rules as shown in Figure 52.

Figure 52

Rather than dividing the range into thirds, access More Rules to set your own percentiles

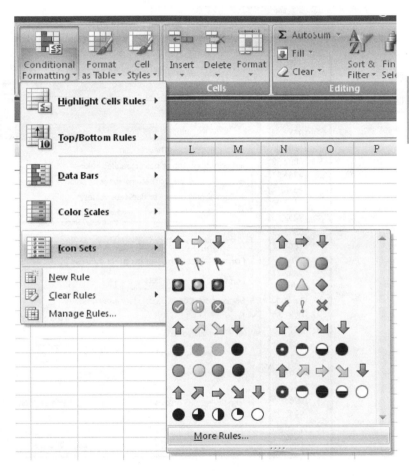

2. In the dialog box, first choose an Icon Style from the bottom dropdown box. This will determine if you have three, four, or five categories.

3. Then, use the Value boxes to set up the percentiles.

The dialog shown in Figure 53 will highlight items in the top and bottom eight percentiles with a green or red arrow.

Figure 53

Using in-cell data bars in Excel 2007

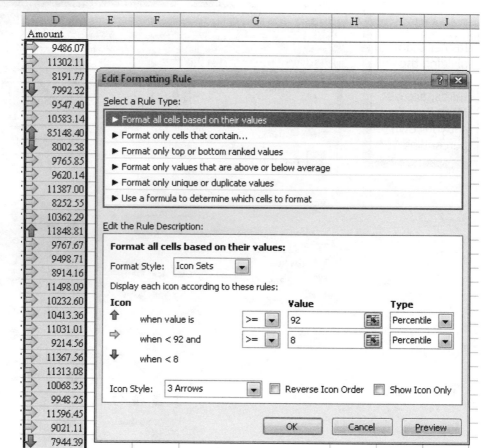

Another new feature in Excel 2007 is the in-cell *Data Bar*.

1. Select a range of numeric data. From the Home ribbon, select
   Conditional Formatting → Data Bars and then choose a color as shown
   in Figure 54.

Figure 54

A Data Bar includes a tiny bar chart in each cell relative to the size of each number

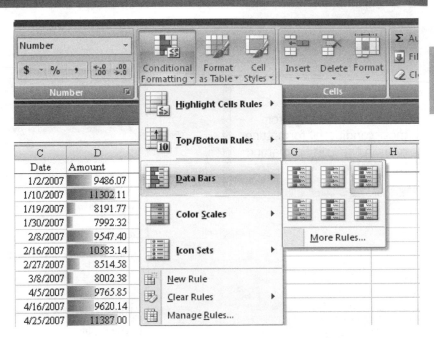

 Tip:

*Do not include a total cell in the range when setting up a data bar. The higher value
in the total will automatically get the largest bar, and will probably make all of the
other bars insignificant.*

The Edit Formatting Rule dialog offers fine-tuning for a conditional formatting rule.

1. From the Conditional Formatting dropdown, choose Manage Rules.

2. Click on a Rule and choose Edit. This will provide you access to a dialog where you can customize the rule.

In Figure 55, the data bar color has been customized and rules have been set up to base the shortest and longest bars on the values at the 10th and 90th percentiles, respectively.

Figure 55

Manage the settings for most conditional formatting rules in the Edit Formatting Rule dialog

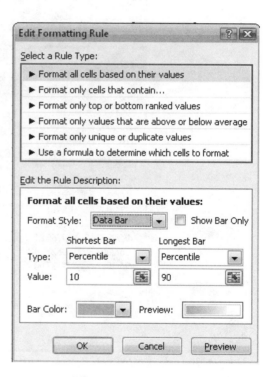

You can apply multiple conditional formatting rules to a range. Use the Manage Rules command to re-sequence the order in which the rules are applied.

Excel Secrets: Applying Icons to Only the Top 10%

When you apply an icon set to a range, one annoyance is that every cell gets an icon, creating a confusing mess. It would be far more powerful to only apply an icon to only the top 10% of the records.

While this does not appear to be possible, you can actually pull this off by setting up a blank formatting rule for the bottom 90% and telling Excel to stop processing rules if the first rule is true. Follow these steps.

1. Set up an icon set for a range using a preset.

2. Use Conditional Formatting → Manage Rules to display the Conditional Formatting Rules Manager.

3. Click the Icon Set rule and choose Edit.

4. Set up a rule similar to Figure 55 above. Indicate that the green arrow should appear for anything at the 89th percentile or above.

5. Click OK to return to the Conditional Formatting Rules Manager.

6. Click New Rule.

7. In the top of the New Formatting Rule dialog, choose Format only top or bottom ranked values. In the Rule Description, choose Bottom from the dropdown. Type 90 in the text box. Click the checkbox for % of the selected range. Do not apply a Format. The dialog should appear as in Figure 56.

Figure 56

Setting up a rule to
format the bottom
90% with no special
formatting or icons

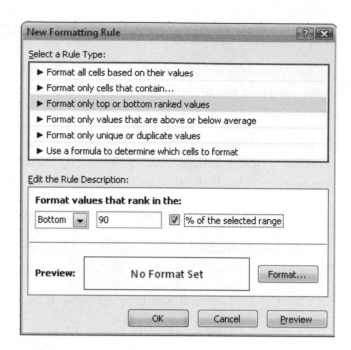

8. Click OK to return
    to the Rules
    Manager.

9. The new rule will be
    above the Icon Set
    rule. On the right
    side, check the Stop
    if True box for the
    new rule as shown
    in Figure 57.

Figure 57   The key is to use the Stop if True setting for the top rule

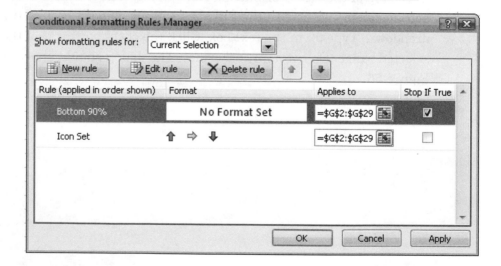

If a cell is in the bottom 90% of the dataset, the "Do Nothing" rule kicks in and no additional rules can be run. Any cells that are not in the bottom 90% then move on to the Icon Set rule, where only the green arrow icon will ever appear, as shown in Figure 58.

Figure 58

This icon set only appears on the top 10% of records

	A	B	C	D	E	F	G
1	Region	CustID	Customer	Qtr	Date	Type	Amount
2	Central	A8239	Unsurpassed Cereal Inc.	Q1	1/2/2007	Services	1193.07
3	Central	A7608	Sure Spring Traders	Q1	1/2/2007	Product	1773.61
4	Central	A7004	Secure Aluminum Partners	Q1	1/2/2007	Product	2099.5
5	Central	A5957	Paramount Luggage Company	Q1	1/2/2007	Product	2252.89
6	Central	A4823	Honest Bottle Inc.	Q1	1/2/2007	Product	3638.5
7	Central	A4924	Ideal Curtain Corporation	Q1	1/2/2007	Product	5009.36
8	Central	A6112	Powerful Sweater Partners	Q1	1/2/2007	Services	10519.23
9	Central	A4312	Functional Valve Company	Q1	1/2/2007	Product	14877.54
10	Central	A3118	Excellent Luggage Inc.	Q1	1/2/2007	Product	⬆ 28658.84
11	East	A5609	Mighty Instrument Inc.	Q1	1/2/2007	Services	2086.44
12	East	A5816	Mouthwatering Leather Company	Q1	1/2/2007	Product	2161.85
13	East	A7181	Special Video Inc.	Q1	1/2/2007	Product	2822.24
14	East	A6004	Persuasive Bolt Corporation	Q1	1/2/2007	Product	3117.12
15	East	A8767	Vivid Tractor Corporation	Q1	1/2/2007	Services	3726.43
16	East	A8826	Wonderful Door Partners	Q1	1/2/2007	Product	4114.09
17	East	A7542	Sure Fruit Supply	Q1	1/2/2007	Product	9008.66
18	East	A7955	Top-Notch Tool Company	Q1	1/2/2007	Services	18654.34
19	East	A2485	Different Film Corporation	Q1	1/2/2007	Product	26893.83
20	East	A1473	Astonishing Crane Company	Q1	1/2/2007	Product	⬆ 43817.8

You could use a similar strategy to apply green data bars to the top 33% and red data bars to the bottom 33% of the records.

Using Conditional Formatting in Excel 2003

Your easy choices are far more limited in Excel 2003 and prior versions.

1. Select a range of numeric data.

2. Select Format → Conditional Format.

3. As shown in Figure 59, you can choose to highlight cells that are greater than a particular number.

Figure 59

Your choices in Excel 2003 are far more limited than in 2007

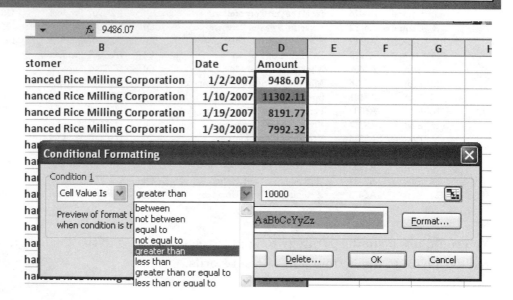

Excel 2003 offers no icon sets, no data bars, no color scales.

In order to highlight cells above the 92% percentile in Excel 2003, you would have to follow these ridiculously hard steps:

1. Select a range of numbers in column D.

2. From the menu, choose Format → Conditional Format.

3. Change the first dropdown to Formula Is.

4. Type a formula such as =D2>PERCENTILE(D:D,0.92).

5. Assign a Format.

6. Click OK.

While Excel gurus could figure out how to build complex formulas such as the one Figure 60, it is certainly beyond the grasp of the average person using Excel.

Figure 60

Although this is possible in Excel 2003, most people would never take the time to figure it out

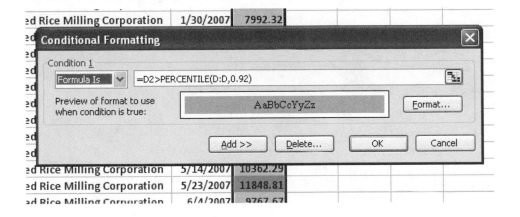

Highlighting
Outliers

Turning Your Data on Its Side with Transpose

If there's one thing that's important in communicating information with data – it's making it LOOK the way you want it to. And Excel doesn't always do that very well.

When you're setting up data to make a table, it will plot rows a certain way – and columns a certain way – but those may not be the ways you want to see them. That's where the option called *Transposing* comes in handy. Transposing literally takes what's currently in a column and shifts it to down to rows or vice versa (takes what's currently in rows and shifts it over into columns).

Turning Data on its Side - Transpose

I'm forever transposing data that I want to put into a table in a specific way.

Here's the Situation

You have a series of dates going down column A. You want these dates to go across row 1.

Here's What to Do

The process of turning a range on its side is called transposing.

1. Select the range containing the dates. Press Ctrl+C to copy.

2. Move to a single blank cell in B1. From the menu, choose Edit → Paste Special. On the Paste Special dialog, choose the Transpose checkbox.

Turning Data on its Side - Transpose

Figure 61

Selecting Transpose from the Paste Special dialog

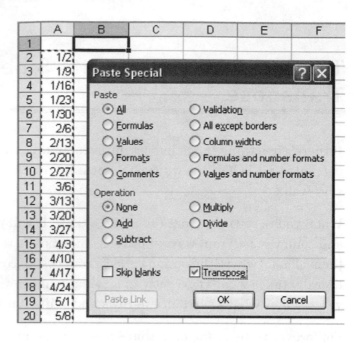

The result: the range is turned from column-wise to row-wise.

Figure 62

Turning a range in its side

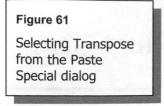

Better in Excel 2007

In Excel 2007, you do not have to access the Paste Special dialog. The Paste dropdown on the Home ribbon offers an option to Transpose.

Figure 63

Selecting Transpose from the Paste dropdown on the Home ribbon

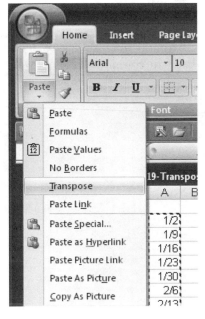

Turning Data on its Side - Transpose

Excel Details

This technique will also work when you want to turn a horizontal range into a vertical range. It will even work with a rectangular range.

 Note:

Strangely enough, Paste Special does not work after using the Cut command. It only works after a Copy command.

Turning Data on its Side - Transpose

Joining Text

Here's the Situation

You are trying to do a lookup between these two datasets. The model number in the lookup table contains "SKU-" before every model. Your dataset has the same models, but is missing the SKU.

Figure 64

Doing a lookup between two datasets

	B	C	D	
	Model	**Date**	**Customer**	**Qu**
	J53	1/1/06	Kroger	
	D18	1/1/06	Wal-Mart	
	B28	1/1/06	Albertson's Inc.	
	J80	1/1/06	ConAgra Foods	
	D22	1/1/06	TransMontaigne	
	C57	1/1/06	Host Marriott Co	
	A65	1/1/06	American Intern	
	I72	1/1/06	Leggett & Platt	
	G52	1/1/06	CIGNA Corp.	
	A16	1/1/06	Triad Hospitals	
	J53	1/1/06	Hughes Supply	
	D18	1/2/06	Wal-Mart	
	B28	1/2/06	Albertson's Inc.	
	J80	1/2/06	Chubb Corp.	
	D22	1/2/06	American Intern	
	C57	1/2/06	The Williams Co	
	A65	1/2/06	PacifiCare Healt	
	I72	1/2/06	Triad Hospitals	

	A	B	C
1	**Model**	**Description**	
2	SKU-A16	8-Bit High Speec	
3	SKU-A65	4 Channel 1 MSI	
4	SKU-B28	2 Channel 200 K	
5	SKU-C46	Single Channel 5	
6	SKU-C57	8-Channel 50 kS	
7	SKU-D18	8-Bit Microproce	
8	SKU-D22	4 Channel 500 kS	
9	SKU-D69	8-Channel 500 kS	
10	SKU-D69	2 Channel 500 kS	
11	SKU-E27	10-Bit 600 ns A/I	
12	SKU-G32	4 Channel 200 kS	
13	SKU-G52	Single Channel 2	
14	SKU-G88	Self-Calibrating I	
15	SKU-H17	1MSPS 8-Bit A/I	
16	SKU-I72	3.3V Self-Calibra	
17	SKU-J53	1MSPS 10-Bit A.	

Here's What to Do

1. To join text, use the Ampersand (&) operator. ="SKU-"&B2 will take care of the problem.

**Joining
Text**

	C2		f_x	="SKU-"&B2	

28-CalculatingText.xls:1

	A	B	C	D
1	Region	Model	SKUModel	Date
2	East	J53	SKU-J53	1/1/06
3	Central	D18	SKU-D18	1/1/06
4	Central	B28	SKU-B28	1/1/06
5	East	J80	SKU-J80	1/1/06
6	West	D22	SKU-D22	1/1/06

Figure 65

Using the Ampersand to join text

2. In the next worksheet, you have an area code in column D and a phone number in column E. Join them using ="("&D2&") "&E2.

Figure 66

Joining an area code and a phone number

	F2		f_x	="("&D2&") "&E2	

	C	D	E	F
1	Address	Area Code	Phone	Telephone
2	1442 Railroad Road, Salem, IL 25677	224	555-5076	(224) 555-5076
3	204 Madison Road, Vienna, IL 52307	224	555-3344	
4	1789 Williams Avenue, Chatham, VT 14823	802	555-2084	
5	541 Franklin Circle, Salem, WV 65773	304	555-1799	

3. Finally, you have first name in column A and last name in column B. The customer's last order date is in column C. Use =A2&B2 to join the first and last names together.

Figure 67

Joining first and last names

4. To build a name with a space between first name and last name, use =A2&" "&B2.

Figure 68

Adding a space between the names

5. With all letters capitalized, the result feels like you are screaming the customer name. Use =PROPER(A2&" "&B2) to generate the names in upper and lower case.

Figure 69

Using PROPER to adjust capitalization for proper names

There is a problem when you want to join text and a date. Although C2 looks like a date, remember that it really contains the number of days since 1/1/1900.

The following formula fails.

=PROPER(A2&" "&B2)&" - thank you for your order on "&C2

Figure 70

Date displayed as number

	A	B	C	D
	D2		*fx*	=PROPER(A2&" "&B2)&" - thank you for your order on "&C2
1	**First Name**	**Last Name**	**Last Date**	
2	DONALD	GOULD	11/1/2005	Donald Gould - thank you for your order on 38657
3	RONALD	CRANE	3/13/2004	Ronald Crane - thank you for your order on 38059

To fix this, use the TEXT function to control the display of the date. You will have to know a custom number format for the desired display of the date. Some examples are "m/d/yy" and "mmm d, yyyy".

Figure 71   Using TEXT to properly display a number as a date

	A	B	C	D	E
	D2		*fx*	=PROPER(A2&" "&B2)&" - thank you for your order on "&TEXT(C2,"mmmm d, yyyy")	
1	**First Name**	**Last Name**	**Last Date**		
2	DONALD	GOULD	11/1/2005	Donald Gould - thank you for your order on November 1, 2005	
3	RONALD	CRANE	3/13/2004	Ronald Crane - thank you for your order on March 13, 2004	
4	MARGARITA	ELLIOTT	12/18/2005	Margarita Elliott - thank you for your order on December 18, 2005	
5	JACQUELINE	ARNOLD	9/2/2003	Jacqueline Arnold - thank you for your order on September 2, 2003	

Looking up Data

Now that you know how to get the data into Excel, you're ready to start looking things up. How many times has this happened to you? You ask for data and – after waiting what seems like forever – there it is. You're on a deadline, the meeting is tomorrow, you need to put together a presentation and some charts. You open the file and ...

Here's the Situation

It happens all the time. Your IT department sends data with customer numbers but no customer name. Or sales rep number without sales rep names. Or you have to match sales from last year to sales for this year.

Figure 72

Data provided with rep numbers but no rep names

	A	B	C	D	E
1	Rep	Date	Acct	Quantity	Revenue
2	66	1/1/06	K9335	114	2901
3	77	1/1/06	W2569	599	12460
4	43	1/1/06	A1780	747	18369
5	87	1/1/06	C3418	118	2943
6	96	1/1/06	T7539	220	4257

Here's What to Do

When this happens, you can usually scare up another table that matches rep numbers with rep names.

Figure 73		A	B	C	D
Table with rep numbers and names	1	Rep	Name	Region	District
	2	23	Carey	West	Seattle
	3	25	Whitaker	East	MidAtlantic
	4	26	Lewis	East	Northeast
	5	43	Castaneda	Central	Midwest
	6	44	Farrell	East	SouthEast

The function to use to add names to the original dataset is the VLOOKUP function. This stands for Vertical Lookup. This is one of the workhorse functions in Excel. It is worthwhile to master it.

In the current example, you have rep numbers from cell A2 through cell A5001. You've copied the table from Figure 73 to cells L2:O24. You want to add rep name in column H. The example will build a formula that can also later be copied to retrieve region and district in columns I and J.

Figure 74   Worksheet with data from two files

	A	B	C	D	E	F	G	H	I	J	K	L	M	N	O
1	Rep	Date	Acct	Quantity	Revenue	COGS	Profit					Rep	Name	Region	District
2	43	1/1/06	A1780	747	18369	10656	7713					23	Carey	West	Seattle
3	57	1/1/06	A9550	1003	23908	14179	9729					25	Whitaker	East	MidAtlantic
4	87	1/1/06	C3418	118	2943	1739	1204					26	Lewis	East	Northeast
5	97	1/1/06	C8711	447	9091	5425	3666					43	Castaneda	Central	Midwest
6	57	1/1/06	H3165	401	8233	5432	2801					44	Farrell	East	SouthEast
7	78	1/1/06	H5372	620	12444	8347	4097					45	Rocha	Central	Texas
8	66	1/1/06	K9335	114	2901	1690	1211					46	Perkins	Central	Texas
9	66	1/1/06	L9036	237	5944	3498	2446					49	Ward	East	Northeast
10	80	1/1/06	T1470	452	8128	5298	2830					52	Dunlap	West	Seattle
11	96	1/1/06	T7539	220	4257	2636	1621					57	Foreman	West	SoCal
12	77	1/1/06	W2569	599	12460	7324	5136					60	Reese	West	SoCal
13	43	1/2/06	A1780	848	14995	9887	5108					61	Strickland	East	MidAtlantic
14	57	1/2/06	A9550	359	7267	4353	2914					66	Nieves	Central	Midwest
15	57	1/2/06	A9550	211	4889	3046	1843					67	Davidson	East	SouthEast
16	57	1/2/06	A9550	580	14566	8553	6013					76	Stout	East	Northeast
17	67	1/2/06	B7437	213	3654	2469	1185					77	Barry	Central	Texas

There are four arguments in the VLOOKUP function.

 The cell containing Rep # for this row

For the formula in H2, this would be $A2.

 Note:

The dollar sign before the A will allow the formula to be copied to I and J.

 A range that contains cell numbers in the left most column and Rep names somewhere in the range

Use $L$2:$O$24. You will want to use dollar signs throughout this reference so that as the formula is copied down to 5000 rows, it always looks back at rows 2:24 to get the rep names.

Looking up Data

 The column number within the above range where the Rep number is located

In this example, column M is the second column in L2:O24.

 The word FALSE

This will prevent Excel from returning close matches.

To fill in the rep name in E, use =VLOOKUP($A2,$L$2:$O$24,2,FALSE).

Figure 75

Using VLOOKUP to obtain RepName

H2	▼		f_x =VLOOKUP($A2,$L$2:$O$24,2,FALSE)				

	A	B	C	D	E	F	G	H
1	Rep	Date	Acct	Quantity	Revenue	COGS	Profit	RepName
2	66	1/1/06	K9335	114	2901	1690	1211	Nieves
3	77	1/1/06	W2569	599	12460	7324	5136	Barry
4	43	1/1/06	A1780	747	18369	10656	7713	Castaneda

Copying the VLOOKUP Formula to Get Region and District

1. Copy the formula in H2 to I2 and J2. Initially, the results will return the rep names again. This is OK.

Figure 76

Copying VLOOKUP formula to Region and District

=VLOOKUP($A2,$L$2:$O$24,2,FALSE)

D	E	F	G	H	I	J
antity	Revenue	COGS	Profit	RepName	Region	District
114	2901	1690	1211	Nieves	Nieves	Nieves
599	12460	7324	5136	Barry		

2. In the Formula bar, edit the third parameter from a 2 to a 3 for cell I2 to obtain the Region. Change this parameter to a 4 in the formula in J2 to obtain the District.

Figure 77

Editing VLOOKUP parameters

=VLOOKUP($A2,$L$2:$O$24,4,FALSE)

VLOOKUP(lookup_value, table_array, **col_index_num**, [range_lookup])

ntity	Revenue	COGS	Profit	RepName	Region	District
114	2901	1690	1211	Nieves	Central	O$24,4,
599	12460	7324	5136	Barry		

The result will return the RepName, Region, and District.

Figure 78

Using VLOOKUP to obtain RepName, Region, and District

=VLOOKUP($A2,$L$2:$O$24,4,FALSE)

	E	F	G	H	I	J
ntity	Revenue	COGS	Profit	RepName	Region	District
114	2901	1690	1211	Nieves	Central	Midwest
599	12460	7324	5136	Barry	Central	Texas
747	18369	10656	7713	Castaneda	Central	Midwest
119	2943	1739	1204	Evans	Central	Midwest

Dealing with #N/A for Missing Values

When Excel can not find a match, the VLOOKUP function returns #N/A. This might happen if the dataset has a number for a new sales rep who is not in your table.

Figure 79   #N/A error message indicates missing value

	A	B	C	D	E	F	G	H	I	J
1	Rep	Date	Acct	Quantity	Revenue	COGS	Profit	RepName	Region	District
2	77	12/31/06	T4596	1126	23473	15308	8165	Barry	Central	Texas
3	77	12/31/06	T4596	102	1863	1203	660	Barry	Central	Texas
4	77	12/31/06	V3507	318	7060	4521	2539	Barry	Central	Texas
5	42	12/31/06	M1831	1010	24682	14768	9914	#N/A	#N/A	#N/A
6	45	12/31/06	C2506	479	8602	5607	2995	Rocha	Central	Texas

Normally, you would sort by column H, so all of the #N/A values would sort to the bottom. You could then add new records to the middle of your lookup table to include the new rep numbers.

However, sometimes you want Excel to return a blank cell when a match is not found. The solution through Excel 2003 is very convoluted.

> You have to check to see if the result is #N/A using the ISNA function.

> You actually have to enter the VLOOKUP function twice in your formula.

Figure 80   Using ISNA and VLOOKUP to return a zero instead of the #N/A error message

`=IF(ISNA(VLOOKUP($A5,$L$2:$O$24,2,FALSE)),"",VLOOKUP($A5,$L$2:$O$24,2,FALSE))`

D	E	F	G	H	I	J	K	L
antity	Revenue	COGS	Profit	RepName	Region	District		Rep
1126	23473	15308	8165	Barry	Central	Texas		23
102	1863	1203	660	Barry	Central	Texas		25
318	7060	4521	2539	Barry	Central	Texas		26
1010	24682	14768	9914					43
479	8602	5607	2995	Rocha	Central	Texas		44

Thankfully, in Excel 2007 or later, this will be replaced with the following streamlined format: =IfError(VLOOKUP($A5,$L$2:$O$24,2,FALSE),"")

When You Know There Is a Match but Excel Cannot Find It

Sometimes, VLOOKUP will not find a match, even though the values look the same. This is often caused by a trailing space or a number stored as text. In the figure below, Excel can find a match for Rep 77 in rows 2 and 4 but not in row 3. If you look at the formula bar for cell A3, you will see that this is actually a number stored as text. Quotation marks are Excel's prefix for a right-aligned text cell.

Figure 81

Quotations before a number in the formula bar indicate that the number is actually text

	A	B	C	G	H	I	J
							A3 ▼ fx "77
1	Rep	Date	Acct	Profit	RepName	Region	District
2	77	12/31/06	T4596	8165	Barry	Central	Texas
3	77	12/31/06	T4596	660			
4	77	12/31/06	V3507	2539	Barry	Central	Texas

If the problem is that one range contains a number and the other range contains text that looks like numbers, then use one of these approaches.

 If the Lookup table contains *numbers* and column A contains *text*, use =VALUE(A2) as the first argument of the VLOOKUP formula.

 If the Lookup table contains *text* and column A contains *numbers*, use =TEXT(A2,"00") as the first argument in the VLOOKUP formula.

Another common problem that occurs when both cells contain text is for one range to contain a trailing space. In Figure 82, cells C3 and M6 look identical, but they are not.

Figure 82

Cells that look alike may differ in the number of trailing spaces

	D2			▼	*fx* =VLOOKUP(C2,$M$2:$N$66,2,FALSE)			
	A	B	C		D	L	M	N
1	Rep	Date	Acct	Customer			Acct	Customer
2	43	1/1/06	A1780	Albertson's Inc.			A6623	Ainsworth
3	57	1/1/06	A9550	#N/A			A3481	Air Canada
4	87	1/1/06	C3418	ConAgra Foods Inc. Omaha			A1780	Albertson's Inc
5	97	1/1/06	C8711	CIGNA Corp.			A5664	Ameren Corp.
6	57	1/1/06	H3165	Hughes Supply Inc.			A9550	American Inter
7	78	1/1/06	H5372	Host Marriott Corp.			A4697	AMR Corp.

Do this with both cells.

1. Select C3 and type the F2 key to put the cell in edit mode. A flashing insertion cursor will appear at the end of the cell value. Is the insertion cursor is flashing immediately after the last character of the Acct number? If not, there are one or more spaces after the value. Check the value in cell M6 of the lookup table.

Figure 83   An insertion point flashing past the last number indicates trailing space(s)

2. To remove the trailing spaces, insert a formula of =TRIM(C2) in an empty column and copy this down. Copy the new column and use Paste → Special → Values to copy the space-less values back over the original column.

Retrieving Many Columns from the Lookup Range

Say that you have to pull 12 monthly values from the Lookup table. Using the method described above, you would have to enter the first VLOOKUP, copy, and then edit the third parameter in the 11 remaining formulas. This could become very tedious.

Use =COLUMN (B2) in place of the "2" as the third parameter. (You chose B2 because it is the second column and the value to return is in the second column of the lookup table). When you copy this formula one column to the right, the reference will change to return the column number of C2, which is 3. This will allow you to quickly enter the formula once and copy it to many columns.

Figure 84

Using COLUMN with VLOOKUP to return several columns

	B2	▼		fx	=VLOOKUP($A2,$AC$2:$AO$34,COLUMN(B2),FALSE)			
	A	B	C	D	E	F	G	H	I
1	Acct	Jan-05	Feb-05	Mar-05	Apr-05	May-05	Jun-05	Jul-05	Au
2	A6623	7464	1190	6599	4405	7598	4582	5055	
3	A3481	0	0	0	0	0	0	0	
4	A1780	4778	4159	6685	7416	1042	7039	2270	

Getting Good Records from Bad Data

Don't you just hate that every auditing task assumes that your data is perfectly formatted and ready to go?! It never is.

You have sales data for the last ten years. Over the course of the ten years, the customer names for many accounts have changed.

It may not be that the customer data is wrong, but a matter that the customer name actually changes during the history of your data. Or more likely, someone in Accounts Receivable had a slow day and decided to neaten up the spelling of the top 20 accounts on a boring day in July 2003.

When you try to produce summaries, you get separate sales for the old name and new name, even though they are the same account.

Figure 85

Data with more than one name for the same account – notice that AOL and AOL Time Warner both have the same account number in column B (A1234)

	A	B	C
1	Date	Acct	Customer
2	3/31/98	A1234	AOL
3	4/12/99	A1234	AOL
4	4/20/00	A1234	AOL Time Warner
5	4/30/01	A1234	AOL Time Warner
6	5/1/02	A1234	AOL Time Warner
7	5/10/03	A1234	AOL Time Warner
8	5/10/04	A1234	AOL Time Warner
9	5/18/05	A1234	AOL Time Warner
10	4/5/98	B2345	Viacom
11	4/12/99	B2345	Viacom
12	4/14/00	B2345	CBS-Viacom
13	4/17/01	B2345	CBS-Viacom
14	4/19/02	B2345	CBS-Viacom
15	5/4/03	B2345	CBS-Viacom
16	5/5/04	B2345	CBS-Viacom
17	5/6/05	B2345	CBS-Viacom

We are going to use the VLOOKUP function to solve this problem.

Figure 86

Using VLOOKUP to make sure all the customer names are consistent

E27 f_x =VLOOKUP(B27,$B$2:$C$33,2,FALSE)

	A	B	C	D	E
1	Date	Acct	Customer	Qty	New Name
2	6/8/05	D4567	Host Marriott Corp.	778	Host Marriott Corp.
3	5/18/05	A1234	AOL Time Warner	237	AOL Time Warner
4	5/17/05	E6543	Cardinal Health, Inc.	108	Cardinal Health, Inc.
5	5/6/05	B2345	CBS-Viacom	237	CBS-Viacom
26	4/17/99	D4567	Host Marriott Corporation	1143	Host Marriott Corp.
27	4/12/99	A1234	AOL	599	AOL Time Warner
28	4/12/99	B2345	Viacom	599	CBS-Viacom
29	4/7/99	E6543	Cardinal Health Inc.	840	Cardinal Health, Inc.
30	4/5/98	B2345	Viacom	114	CBS-Viacom
31	4/5/98	D4567	Host Marriott Corporation	1064	Host Marriott Corp.
32	4/5/98	E6543	Cardinal Health Inc.	1148	Cardinal Health, Inc.
33	3/31/98	A1234	AOL	114	AOL Time Warner
34					

The formula in row 27 says, "Go look through column B and find a cell equal to B27 (A1234). When you find it, tell me the name in that row." The first record for AOL Time Warner is in row 3, and since we've put the most recent names at the top, it happens to have the AOL Time Warner Name.

 Note:

It is important that you sort the data in descending order by Date. This will put the most recent (and in theory, the "best") customer name at the top of the list.

In other words, the VLOOKUP function looks for a match to the account number in B2. It stops as soon as it finds the first match from the top. Thus, using =VLOOKUP(B27,$B$2:$C$33,2,FALSE) will change all of the customer names for account number A1234 to the same name.

 Note:

Remember to Copy and Paste Special Values in the new column to freeze the results.

VLOOKUPs Take a Long Time to Calculate

In the case above, you are really doing 24 VLOOKUPs in each row. This seems unnecessary, because once Excel has found the correct row number in the first formula, it should be able to use this for the rest of the lookups in the row.

There is a function called MATCH. It works like VLOOKUP, but instead of returning a value from the lookup table, it returns the row number within the range where the matching value is found.

In Figure 87, Excel looks for T7539 in the range of AF2:AF66. The value is found in cell AF60, which is the 59th row in the range.

Figure 87

Using the MATCH function

| | B2 | | | ▼ | | *fx* | =MATCH(A2,$AF$2:$AF$66,FALSE) |

	A	B	C	D	E	F	G
1	Acct	Row	Jan-05	Feb-05	Mar-05	Apr-05	May-0
2	T7539	59					
3	I6286	30					
4	U3237	61					
5	T7654	55					

At first, this seems like useless information! The first time that I found the MATCH function I dismissed it – why would anyone care that the match is on the 59th row? However, see what happens when you combine this with another seemingly useless function, INDEX. =INDEX(AG2:AG66,59,1) returns the 59th row and first column of AG2:AG66. Again – this seems useless until you put the results of the MATCH function as the second argument of the INDEX function.

Figure 88

Using the INDEX function

| | C2 | | | ▼ | | *fx* | =INDEX(AG$2:AG$66,$B2) |

	A	B	C	D	E	F
1	Acct	Row	Jan-05	Feb-05	Mar-05	Apr-0
2	T7539	59	867			
3	I6286	30				
4	U3237	61				
5	T7654	55				

The advantage? VLOOKUP is processor-intensive. By using one MATCH per row and then 12 INDEX functions per row, worksheet calculation time will dramatically improve.

Sometimes, your key field is not in the left column of the Lookup table. Many times, it is easier to move the columns in the lookup table around, but it is also possible to craft a solution using INDEX and MATCH.

Figure 89

Combining INDEX and MATCH

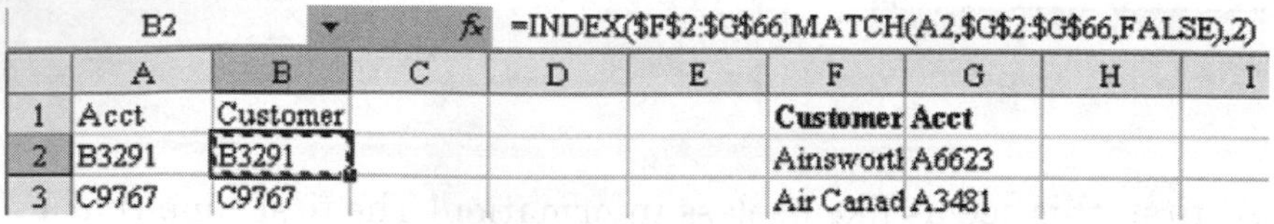

B2			▼	*fx*	=INDEX($F$2:$G$66,MATCH(A2,$G$2:$G$66,FALSE),2)			
	A	B	C	D	E	F	G	H	I
1	Acct	Customer				**Customer**	**Acct**		
2	B3291	B3291				Ainsworth	A6623		
3	C9767	C9767				Air Canad	A3481		

Sorting Your Data

Here's the Situation

Everyone sorts data, but there are some tricks that you can use to make your sorting easier:

- Sorting Data with One Click
- Sorting into a Custom Sequence
- Sorting by Color (new in Excel 2007!)
- Sorting on more than three fields using the More Sort option

Here's What to Do

You can quickly sort data with one click, but it is important to understand the rules for trouble-free sorting.

Sorting Data with One Click

When you sort using the AZ or ZA buttons in the Standard toolbar or Data ribbon, you are relying on Excel's to accurately find the correct range to sort and to identify that you have headings above the data.

1. Make sure that every column in your data has a one-cell heading above the data.
   This is important. It is very common to add a new column to the end with a formula and to forget to put a heading above this column. When Excel encounters a blank cell at the top of just one column, the

IntelliSense assumes that you have no headings and sorts the top row down into your data. Make sure to fill in every heading and you will not have this problem.

2. To sort, select a single cell in the column.

   Do not select the whole column. Do not select two cells. Select just one cell. If you select more than one cell, Excel will think that you want to sort just the selected range. This will lead to disastrous results.

Figure 90

Never select an entire column to sort

	C	D	E	F	G	H
1	Date	Customer	Quantity	Revenue	COGS	Profit
2	1-Jan-04	Ford	1000	22810	10220	12590
3	2-Jan-04	Verizon	100	2257	984	1273
4	2-Jan-04	Verizon	500	10245	4235	6010
5	3-Jan-04	Ainsworth	500	11240	5110	6130
6	4-Jan-04	Ainsworth	400	9204	4088	5116
7	4-Jan-04	Gildan Activewe	800	18552	7872	10680

3. Once you have selected one column, press the AZ button to sort in ascending order or the ZA button to sort in descending order. In the following figure, cell F2 is selected. When you press the ZA button, the dataset will be sorted with the largest sales at the top.

 Note:

When you need to sort one field within another, do the inner sort first. For example, say that you want the data sorted by region. Within each region, the customers should be in alphabetic sequence. Within each customer, the data should be in date sequence. You can complete this sort in six clicks of the mouse. See below.

Figure 91

Selecting a single cell to sort and clicking ZA to sort descending

E	F	G	H
Quantity	**Revenue**	**COGS**	**Profit**
1000	22810	10220	12590
100	2257	984	1273
500	10245	4235	6010

4. Click any one cell in the Date column.

5. Click the AZ button to sort by date.

6. Select one cell in the Customer column.

7. Click the AZ button.
    The data will be sorted by customer. When a tie is encountered, the previous sort order will be retained, resulting in the prior Date sort remaining within each customer as shown below.

Sorting Your Data

Figure 92

After sorting by Customer, the original date sort is used to break ties

	A	B	C	D
1	**Region**	**Product**	**Date**	**Customer**
2	Central	XYZ	3-Jan-04	Ainsworth
3	Central	XYZ	4-Jan-04	Ainsworth
4	East	XYZ	10-Jan-04	Ainsworth
5	West	XYZ	12-Jan-04	Ainsworth

8. Select a cell in the Region column.

9. Click AZ to complete the sort. The data will now be sorted by Date within Customer within Region.

Figure 93

Sorted data

	A	B	C	D
1	**Region**	**Product**	**Date**	**Customer**
144	Central	XYZ	8-Dec-04	P&G
145	Central	XYZ	27-Feb-04	Phillip Morris
146	Central	ABC	16-Oct-04	Phillip Morris
147	Central	DEF	18-Jun-04	SBC Communic
148	Central	XYZ	10-Jul-04	Sears

Note:

In the rare case where you have a narrow dataset and a numeric heading, you will have to apply bold format to the heading in order to prevent the heading from sorting into the data.

Gotcha

Having one blank cell in the heading will usually cause the headings to be sorted into the data. This would cause the Region heading to move to row 411, just between values for "East" and "West". If you see your headings disappear after a sort, press Ctrl+Z to undo.

Here's the Situation

Any consumer can tell that the new model 1100 must be better than the old model 900. However, Excel will treat this data as text and sort "Model 1100" before "Model 900".

A similar opportunity is where your company's custom is to sort regions into a sequence of East, Central, West. There is not a standard sort order that will cause the East region to sort first.

Here's What to Do

Sorting in a Custom Sequence

It is easy to add a custom list to Excel on your computer. You will then be able to use a custom sort sequence to have the products sort into the proper sequence.

1. In a blank region of a worksheet, type the regions or products in the proper sequence. Select the range containing this list.
   In Excel 97-2003: Select Tools → Options. In the Options dialog, choose the tab for Custom Lists.
   In Excel 2007: Choose Office Icon → Excel Options → Personalize. In the section "Top options for Working With Excel", click the Edit Custom Lists... button.

2. Provided that you selected your list before invoking the command, the range will be pre-entered in the Import List from Cells box. Ensure this is the correct range and choose the Import button.

Figure 94

Configuring and importing a new custom list in the desired order

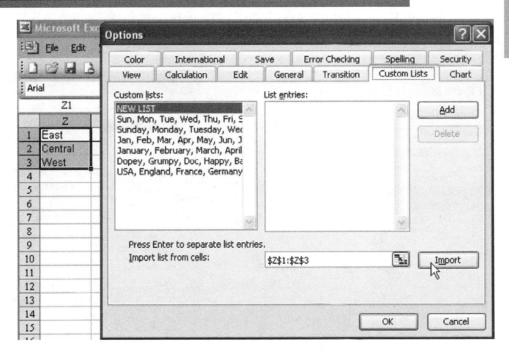

The new list is imported to the list of Custom lists on this computer. You only have to import the list once per computer. The list will be available to you in the future on this computer.

Figure 95

New custom list appears in the Custom lists

3. When you need to sort regions using this custom sequence, you will have to use the Sort dialog instead of the AZ or ZA buttons. Select a cell in your data. From the menu, select Data → Sort.

4. In the Excel 97-2003 Sort dialog, choose to sort by Region. Then, press the Options button in the lower left corner of the dialog.

Figure 96

Choosing Options to reach the custom sort options

5. In the Excel 97-2003 Sort Options dialog, choose the dropdown next to Normal and choose your new custom list as the sequence. Note that this custom sort sequence only applies to the first sort key.

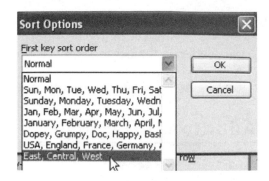

Figure 97

Selecting the new custom sort

6. Click OK to return to the Sort dialog.

7. In Excel 2007, click the Sort icon in the Data Ribbon. For Sort by, Choose Region. For Sort On, choose Values. In the Order dropdown, choose Custom List... and then select East, Central, West.

Figure 98

Selecting the desired order to sort by

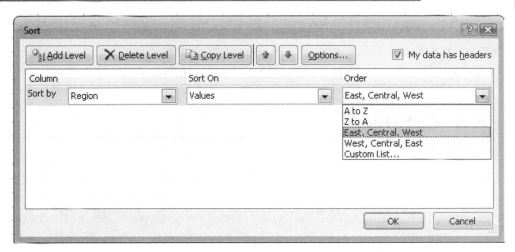

8. Click OK to sort the data. The result is that the East region now appears first.

	A	B	C
1	**Region**	**Product**	**Date**
2	East	ABC	4-Nov-04
3	East	ABC	23-Apr-04
4	East	ABC	17-Jul-04

Figure 99

Data sorted in the desired East, Central, West order

Additional Details

In Excel 97-2003, there is a shortcut if you only have one custom sort field. After doing the first sort with the Sort dialog, Excel will remember the East, Central, West setting. You can now do subsequent sorts using the AZ button on the Standard Toolbar. However, if you need to sort Region in a custom sequence and Country in another custom sequence, you will be forced to keep using the Sort dialog box.

Gotcha

In Excel 97-2003, if you need to sort by Region within Product, you would have to first use the Sort dialog to do a custom sort on Region. Then, do a second sort to sort by Product.

Excel Details

Custom lists are also used for extending a series with the fill handle. Type any entry from your list in a blank cell. Grab the fill handle and drag to fill in the remaining items from your list. The fill handle is the square dot in the lower right corner of the selected cell.

Better in Excel 2007 – Sorting by Color

The Sort dialog in Excel 2007 offers fantastic functionality. You can now sort by color, sort by icon, or sort by values.

The process of sorting by color is a bit cumbersome, but it is certainly possible.

In Figure 100, three fill colors are used in the customer field in order to stratify the records, based on responsibility. An icon set is applied to the top 90% of the records in column G.

Figure 100

Customer records were manually marked with colors

	A	B	C	D	E	F	G
1	Region	CustID	Customer	Qtr	Date	Type	Amount
2	West	A1343	Appealing Mining Supply	Q1	1/2/2007	Product	2148.81
3	East	A1473	Astonishing Crane Company	Q1	1/2/2007	Product	43817.8
4	East	A2485	Different Film Corporation	Q1	1/2/2007	Product	26893.83
5	West	A3045	Enhanced Telephone Inc.	Q1	1/2/2007	Product	6910.78
6	Central	A3118	Excellent Luggage Inc.	Q1	1/2/2007	Product	28658.84
7	Central	A4312	Functional Valve Company	Q1	1/2/2007	Product	14877.54
8	Central	A4823	Honest Bottle Inc.	Q1	1/2/2007	Product	3638.5
9	Central	A4924	Ideal Curtain Corporation	Q1	1/2/2007	Product	5009.36
10	West	A4985	Improved Crane Company	Q1	1/2/2007	Product	3183.62
11	East	A5609	Mighty Instrument Inc.	Q1	1/2/2007	Services	2086.44
12	East	A5816	Mouthwatering Leather Company	Q1	1/2/2007	Product	2161.85
13	Central	A5957	Paramount Luggage Company	Q1	1/2/2007	Product	2252.89
14	West	A5972	Paramount Machinery Company	Q1	1/2/2007	Product	6202.29
15	East	A6004	Persuasive Bolt Corporation	Q1	1/2/2007	Product	3117.12
16	Central	A6112	Powerful Sweater Partners	Q1	1/2/2007	Services	10519.23
17	Central	A7004	Secure Aluminum Partners	Q1	1/2/2007	Product	2099.5
18	West	A7054	Secure Plywood Company	Q1	1/2/2007	Product	2779.58
19	East	A7181	Special Video Inc.	Q1	1/2/2007	Product	2822.24
20	West	A7429	Supreme Bottle Supply	Q1	1/2/2007	Services	2845.66
21	East	A7542	Sure Fruit Supply	Q1	1/2/2007	Product	9008.66
22	Central	A7608	Sure Spring Traders	Q1	1/2/2007	Product	1773.61
23	East	A7955	Top-Notch Tool Company	Q1	1/2/2007	Services	18654.34
24	West	A8185	Trustworthy Tool Corporation	Q1	1/2/2007	Product	54612.61
25	Central	A8239	Unsurpassed Cereal Inc.	Q1	1/2/2007	Services	1193.07
26	West	A8390	Unsurpassed Utensil Inc.	Q1	1/2/2007	Product	16255.87
27	West	A8553	User-Friendly Iron Supply	Q1	1/2/2007	Product	23131.67
28	East	A8767	Vivid Tractor Corporation	Q1	1/2/2007	Services	3726.43
29	East	A8826	Wonderful Door Partners	Q1	1/2/2007	Product	4114.09

The goal is to sort by color in column C and, within each color, to have the green arrow icons appear at the top. If there are no icons, the records should be sorted alphabetically. Follow these steps:

1. Select a single cell in the data.

2. From the Data ribbon, click the Sort icon as shown here.

Figure 101

Use the icon with the word "Sort" to access the powerful Sort dialog.

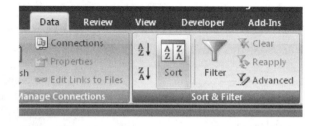

3. For the first sort level, choose Sort by Customer, Sort On Cell Color, and choose the darkest color on top.

Figure 102

Each color requires another sorting level

4. Click Add Level.

5. Repeat Steps 3 and 4 for the other colors in the customer column.

6. Click Add Level.

7. Choose Then by Amount, Sort On Cell Icon, Green Arrow On Top.

8. Click Add Level.

9. Choose Then by Customer, Sort on Values, A to Z. The Sort dialog should appear as below.

Figure 103

Ready to sort

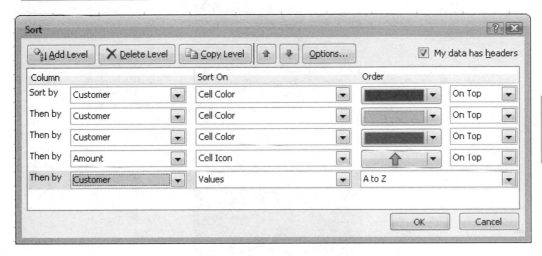

10. Click OK to Sort. The data will be sorted with the green arrows at the top of each color section, as shown below.

Figure 104

Data is sorted by color

◢	A	B	C	D	E	F	G
1	Region	CustID	Customer	Qtr	Date	Type	Amount
2	East	A5609	Mighty Instrument Inc.	Q1	1/2/2007	Services	2086.44
3	East	A5816	Mouthwatering Leather Company	Q1	1/2/2007	Product	2161.85
4	East	A6004	Persuasive Bolt Corporation	Q1	1/2/2007	Product	3117.12
5	East	A7181	Special Video Inc.	Q1	1/2/2007	Product	2822.24
6	East	A7542	Sure Fruit Supply	Q1	1/2/2007	Product	9008.66
7	East	A7955	Top-Notch Tool Company	Q1	1/2/2007	Services	18654.34
8	East	A8767	Vivid Tractor Corporation	Q1	1/2/2007	Services	3726.43
9	East	A8826	Wonderful Door Partners	Q1	1/2/2007	Product	4114.09
10	East	A1473	Astonishing Crane Company	Q1	1/2/2007	Product	⬆ 43817.8
11	West	A8185	Trustworthy Tool Corporation	Q1	1/2/2007	Product	⬆ 54612.61
12	West	A1343	Appealing Mining Supply	Q1	1/2/2007	Product	2148.81
13	East	A2485	Different Film Corporation	Q1	1/2/2007	Product	26893.83
14	West	A3045	Enhanced Telephone Inc.	Q1	1/2/2007	Product	6910.78
15	West	A4985	Improved Crane Company	Q1	1/2/2007	Product	3183.62
16	West	A5972	Paramount Machinery Company	Q1	1/2/2007	Product	6202.29
17	West	A7054	Secure Plywood Company	Q1	1/2/2007	Product	2779.58
18	West	A7429	Supreme Bottle Supply	Q1	1/2/2007	Services	2845.66
19	West	A8390	Unsurpassed Utensil Inc.	Q1	1/2/2007	Product	16255.87
20	West	A8553	User-Friendly Iron Supply	Q1	1/2/2007	Product	23131.67
21	Central	A3118	Excellent Luggage Inc.	Q1	1/2/2007	Product	⬆ 28658.84
22	Central	A4312	Functional Valve Company	Q1	1/2/2007	Product	14877.54
23	Central	A4823	Honest Bottle Inc.	Q1	1/2/2007	Product	3638.5
24	Central	A4924	Ideal Curtain Corporation	Q1	1/2/2007	Product	5009.36
25	Central	A5957	Paramount Luggage Company	Q1	1/2/2007	Product	2252.89
26	Central	A6112	Powerful Sweater Partners	Q1	1/2/2007	Services	10519.23
27	Central	A7004	Secure Aluminum Partners	Q1	1/2/2007	Product	2099.5
28	Central	A7608	Sure Spring Traders	Q1	1/2/2007	Product	1773.61
29	Central	A8239	Unsurpassed Cereal Inc.	Q1	1/2/2007	Services	1193.07

Dealing with Dates

Here's the Situation

Excel can frustrate you when it comes to dates. You might have real dates in Excel, do a calculation, and then get results that appear wrong because the resultant cells have the wrong numeric format. Or, you might have dates that look like real dates, but are really text. These always look good, but they never calculate correctly.

Here's What to Do

Excel stores dates as the number of days since January 1, 1900. When you enter a date such as 6/17/2006, Excel converts it to the number 38885 and then formats the cell to display this number as a date.

Calculating with Dates

1. Try this – enter 39878 in any cell. Select the cell. Choose Format → Cells from the menu. On the Format dialog, go to the Number tab. Choose a date format. Excel will display this number as March 6, 2009.

Figure 105

Formatting a number as a date

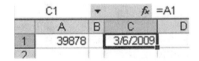

2. Excel stores times as a decimal portion of a day. Try entering 0.75 in a cell and then formatting the cell with a time format. The cell will appear as 6PM.

Excel uses this method of storing dates as numbers in order to make date arithmetic possible.

3. Enter your next birthday in cell A1. In cell A2, enter =A1–TODAY(). The result should tell you how many days until your next birthday. The problem is that sometimes Excel's IntelliSense will format the result as a date. 78 days from January 1, 1900 is a day in the middle of March.

Figure 106

Unexpected results when subtracting with dates

	A2		▾		*fx* =A1-TODAY()	
	A	B	C		D	
1	2/17/2006					
2	3/18/1900					
3						

4. Select this cell and format it as a number; you will see the result is 78 days. This is a situation where Excel performed the right calculation but used the wrong formatting, which made it initially appear wrong.

Figure 107

Formatting the result as a date provides the expected result

	A2		▾		*fx* =A1-TODAY()	
	A	B	C		D	
1	2/17/2006					
2	78					
3						

5. In cell A3, type Ctrl+; to enter today's date. To find the last day of this month, enter
    = DATE(YEAR(A3),MONTH(A3)+1,1)-1 in cell A4.

Figure 108

Finding the last day of the month

	A4		▾		*fx* =DATE(YEAR(A3),MONTH(A3)+1,1)-1			
	A	B	C	D	E	F	C
3	12/1/2005						
4	12/31/2005						

Converting Text That Looks Like a Date to a Real Date

If a calculation on a date returns 0 or a #VALUE! error, it is possible that the cell contains a text that looks like a date. It is worth your time to spend a couple of minutes to try to convert this information to real dates. If the format of the text cells happens to be one that Excel can recognize, you can use the DateValue function to convert the text dates to real dates.

This figure shows which cells work and which do not. The only difference between the format in row 20 that works and the format in row 17 that doesn't work is a comma after the month.

Figure 109

Dealing with zero and #VALUE errors

C14			fx =DATEVALUE(A14)	
	A	B	C	D
14	1/25/2005		1/25/05	
15	1-25-2005		1/25/05	
16	1-Jan-2005		1/1/05	
17	Jan 25 2005		#VALUE!	
18	January 25, 2005		1/25/05	
19	Jan-1-2005		#VALUE!	
20	Jan 25, 2005		1/25/05	
21	2005 Jan, 25		#VALUE!	
22	01-25-2005		1/25/05	
23	25-01-2005		#VALUE!	

Dealing w/ Dates

Fiscal Responsibility (Fiscal Years NOT Ending on 12/31)

Excel does a horrible job dealing with data where the fiscal year end is not 12/31. Excel offers functions that can group by year and quarter, but all of these assume that your fiscal year ends December 31.

Figure 110

Excel assumes fiscal years end on 12/31

D2 =YEAR(C2)

	A	B	C	D	
1	**Region**	**Product**	**Date**	**Year**	C
2	East	XYZ	2/7/07	2007	k
3	Central	ABC	8/24/05	2005	V
4	Central	DEF	11/4/06	2006	A
5	East	XYZ	5/8/05	2005	C
6	West	ABC	8/18/06	2006	T
7	West	DEF	5/4/05	2005	H
8	West	DEF	4/1/06	2006	A

Say that your fiscal year ends March 31. Thus, all dates from April 1, 2006 through March 31, 2007 are classified as fiscal year 2007.

The MONTH function will return a month number from 1 to 12. The YEAR function will return the calendar year. The basic logic then, is that the fiscal year is equal to the year if the month is ≤ 3. Otherwise, the fiscal year is the calendar year + 1.

You can write an IF function to handle this:
=IF(MONTH(C2)<=3,YEAR(C2),1+YEAR(C2))

Figure 111

Using IF, MONTH, and YEAR to deal with fiscal years that do not end on 12/31

D2 =IF(MONTH(C2)<=3,YEAR(C2),1+YEAR(C2))

	A	B	C	D	E	F	
1	**Region**	**Product**	**Date**	**Year**	**Customer**	**Quantity**	**Re**
2	East	XYZ	2/7/07	2007	Kroger	114	
3	Central	ABC	8/24/05	2006	Wal-Mart	599	
4	Central	DEF	11/4/06	2007	Albertson's Inc.	747	

Analyzing Data with Pivot Tables

Here's the Situation

Pivot tables are the most powerful feature in Excel. With a pivot table, you can easily summarize 500,000 rows of data with a few mouse clicks. You can drill down to see more detail, or pivot the report to get another view of the data. Pivot tables allow you to group, compare, contrast, and start seeing patterns.

Here's What to Do

Preparing Your Data

Analyzing w/ PivotTables

Pivot tables should be created on datasets of transactional data. Transactional data has numeric fields such as quantity, revenue, and cost as well as identifying data such as date, customer, or product. Each field should be in a column. If a column contains quantity, there should be nothing else in the column except for a heading and many quantity values.

Figure 112 is perfect for pivot tables. Each row represents a single sale of a product to a customer on a specific date.

Figure 112

Dataset well-suited to the creation of a pivot table

	A	B	C	D	E	F	G
1	**Product**	**Date**	**Customer**	**Quantity**	**Revenue**	**COGS**	**Profit**
2	Model 500	12/31/06	New Instrument	583	10254	6113	4141
3	Model 600	12/31/06	Distinctive Valve	963	18336	11457	6879
4	Model 700	12/31/06	Innovative Pavin	829	17396	11855	5541
5	Model 300	12/31/06	Colossal Instrur	522	10306	5341	4965
6	Model 300	12/30/06	Innovative Pavin	315	5811	3158	2653
7	Model 500	12/30/06	Handy Cereal In	510	11444	6370	5074
8	Model 500	12/30/06	Innovative Pavin	959	20315	12118	8197
9	Model 600	12/29/06	Innovative Pavin	910	20797	13053	7744
10	Model 600	12/29/06	Colossal Crane	346	8282	5034	3248

The layout shown below is not suitable for pivot tables. Months should not span several columns. Column D contains quantity, revenue, COGS, and profit. Blank cells in A3:A9 are presumably for the same customer as in A2, but Excel can not deal with this concept.

If you have data like this, go back to your I.T. department to see if they can generate the raw transactional data that was used to create this summary.

Figure 113

This data is not suitable for pivot tables

	A	B	C	D	E	F
1	Customer	Product	Data	Jan-06	Feb-06	Mar-06
2	New Instrument Company	Model 100	Quantity	2329	539	907
3			Revenue	43067	10319	19655
4			COGS	30279	7089	13086
5			Profit	12788	3230	6569
6		Model 200	Quantity	1663	835	
7			Revenue	34218	17813	
8			COGS	22279	12570	
9			Profit	11939	5243	
10	Distinctive Valve Company	Model 100	Quantity	1962		1024
11			Revenue	43596		24082
12			COGS	28848		15543
13			Profit	14748		8539

Creating a Summary with a Pivot Table

You have 5000 rows of data representing sales over a ten year period. You want to determine trends and be able to drill into the data.

Figure 114

Dataset with ten years of records that you need to summarize

	A	B	C	D	E	F	G
1	Product	Date	Customer	Quantity	Revenue	COGS	Profit
2	Model 500	12/31/06	New Instrument	583	10254	6113	4141
3	Model 600	12/31/06	Distinctive Valve	963	18336	11457	6879
4	Model 700	12/31/06	Innovative Pavin	829	17396	11855	5541
5	Model 300	12/31/06	Colossal Instrur	522	10306	5341	4965
6	Model 300	12/30/06	Innovative Pavin	315	5811	3158	2653
7	Model 500	12/30/06	Handy Cereal In	510	11444	6370	5074
8	Model 500	12/30/06	Innovative Pavin	959	20315	12118	8197
9	Model 600	12/29/06	Innovative Pavin	910	20797	13053	7744
10	Model 600	12/29/06	Colossal Crane	346	8282	5034	3248

Pivot tables offer incredible power to a variety of summary analyses. This feature is the most powerful tool in the toolkit of any auditor.

Pivot tables allow you to quickly produce any of these summaries, plus others:

> ➢ What products are we selling
>
> ➢ Which customers are buying our products
>
> ➢ Which products are being bought by which customers
>
> ➢ Are product sales trending up or down over time

Creating Your First Pivot Table in Excel 97-2003

1. Make sure that your data contains a unique one-cell heading above each column. Select one cell in the data. From the menu, select Data → PivotTable and PivotChart Report.

2. In Step 1 of the Wizard, accept the default selections that your data is in Excel and that you are creating a pivot table.

Figure 115 PivotTable Wizard showing default settings

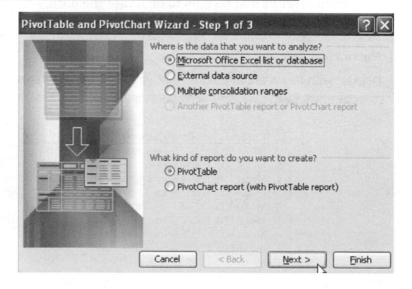

Analyzing w/
PivotTables

3. In Step 2 of the Wizard, confirm that Excel has chosen the right data source for your pivot table.

Figure 116

Confirming data source

4. For your first pivot table, choose the Layout button in step 3.

Figure 117

Selecting the Layout button in Step 3

Analyzing w/ PivotTables

 Note:

In Excel 97 and before, the Wizard was four steps long. Step 3 required you to do the steps on the Layout dialog.

The Layout dialog allows you to build your report by dragging and dropping. It is a blank canvas. Notice that your field list is on the right side. On the left side, there are four areas of the pivot table, waiting for you to drag fields to them.

Figure 118

Using the Layout screen to drag and drop fields

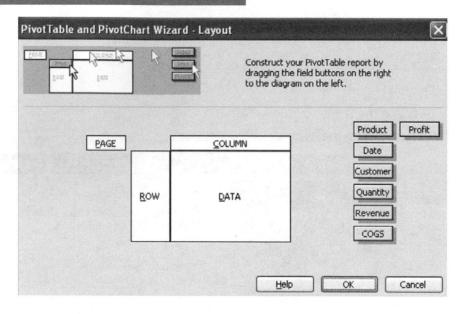

For your first pivot table, get a summary of sales by product.

You have some choices. Do you want to see unit sales (Quantity) or revenue? Drag either field and drop it in the Data area of the dialog.

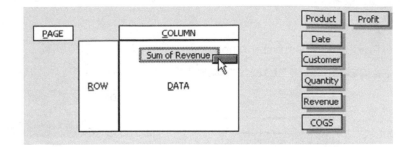

Figure 119

Producing a summary of sales by product

5. Next – do you want the product list going down the side of the report or across the top of the report? If you want the product list going down the side, then drag the Product field to the Row section of the dialog. If you want products going across the top, drag the product field to the Column area of the layout.

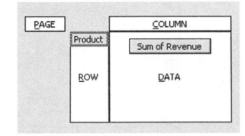

Figure 120

Position of fields in which product list will go down

The preceding layout will create a report with products going down the rows of column A and the total revenue dollars for each product in the heart of the report. This is a very basic but useful report. Go with this pivot table as your first – it is easy to add new fields once the pivot table is created.

6. Click OK to return to the Pivot Table Wizard. In Step 3 of the wizard, choose to have the pivot table created on a new worksheet and click Finish.

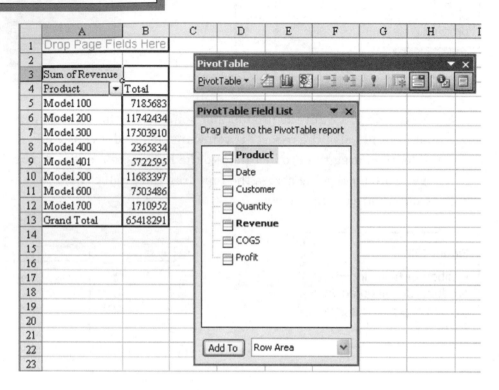

Figure 121

Producing a summary report

In seconds, your summary report will be presented on a new worksheet.

Whenever you select a cell within the pivot table report, the PivotTable Field List will appear. It has looked different in every version of Excel. In early versions of Excel, it was part of the PivotTable toolbar. Later, it became its own floating pane. If the PivotTable Field List disappears, you have selected a cell outside of the range of the pivot table. Select a cell inside the pivot table to bring it back.

Analyzing w/
PivotTables

Figure 122

Select PivotTable Wizard from the PivotTable toolbar dropdown to return to the wizard

If you are comfortable using the Layout dialog to change the pivot table, the first dropdown on the PivotTable toolbar will allow you to go back to the PivotTable Wizard.

Analyzing w/
PivotTables

Creating Your First PivotTable in Excel 2007

To create a similar pivot table in Excel 2007, follow these steps.

1. Select a cell in the dataset.

2. From the Insert ribbon, choose the PivotTable icon.

Figure 124

Creating a
PivotTable
in Excel
2007

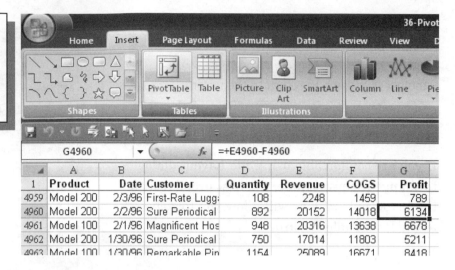

3. In the Create PivotTable dialog, click OK.

Figure 123

Selecting the dataset to be used for the pivot table

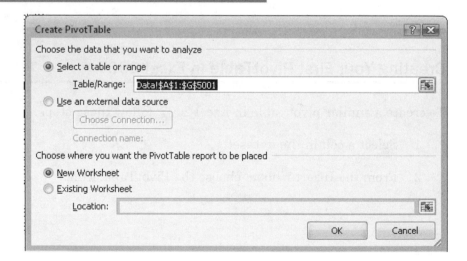

4. In the top half of the PivotTable Field List, checkmark Product and
    Revenue. Excel's IntelliSense will put the fields in the right location.

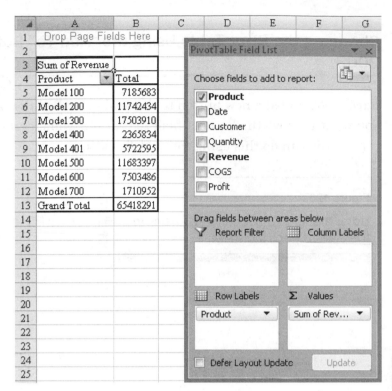

Figure 125

Selecting
fields to
include in the
PivotTable
report

Analyzing w/
PivotTables

Changing the Pivot Table Using the "Add To" Button in Excel 97-2003

Excel 2002 added a new button to the field list called the "Add To" button. If you want to move the Product field so that it is going across the top row of the report, you can do this using the Add To button.

Figure 126

Using the Add To button to add fields to the desired pivot table area

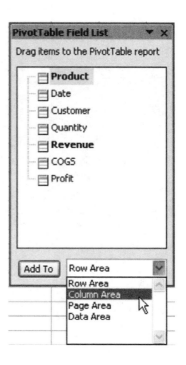

1. First, select the Product field in the field list. Then use the dropdown to change Row area to Column area.

2. When you press the Add To button, the report will change to show the products going across the top of the report.

Figure 127

Selecting Column area

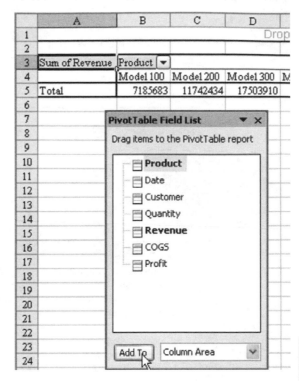

You can use this method to add new fields to the report. Choose the Customer field and add it to the Row area. You will have a report with customers going down column A and products going across the top.

Figure 128

Selecting Customer field and Row area

	A	B	C	D	E	F
1				Drop Page Fields Here		
2						
3	Sum of Revenue	Product ▼				
4	Customer ▼	Model 100	Model 200	Model 300	Model 400	Model 401
5	Agile Sweater Inc.			50956		
6	Alluring Dog Food Corporation	216282	194800	549921	98078	20015
7	Appealing Cutlery Corporation		13972	559214	26259	16621
8	Astonishing Clock Company		23611	294780	90409	17482
9	Beautiful Boiler Corporation	233040	2			3728
10	Beautiful Control Corporation					3856
11	Best Stamping Traders	47717	1			1422
12	Colossal Crane Supply					
13	Colossal Instrument Corporation	85078	2			2198
14	Crisp Stamping Inc.	40718	4			6105
15	Distinctive Valve Company	175234	2			2611
16	Excellent Hosiery Inc.	186122	2			3735
17	Exclusive Bolt Inc.	346722	6			
18	Exclusive Fabric Corporation	266668	9			
19	Exclusive Periodical Company					2350
20	Fascinating Fruit Corporation	36896				4394
21	Fascinating Pharmaceutical Company	6686				2433
22	Fashionable Apparel Corporation					0466
23	First-Rate Luggage Company	495294	4			
24	Forceful Apparel Inc.					
25	Friendly Juice Corporation					
26	Friendly Luggage Corporation					
27	Fully Film Corporation					

PivotTable Field List ▼ ✕

Drag items to the PivotTable report

- **Product**
- Date
- **Customer**
- Quantity
- **Revenue**
- COGS
- Profit

[Add To] Row Area ▼

Analyzing w/
PivotTables

Changing the Pivot Table in Excel 2007

In Excel 2007, you can drag fields in the PivotTable Field List dialog. Drag Product from the Row Labels section to the Column Labels section.

To add a new field, simply click the checkbox in the top of the PivotTable Field List dialog. In the Figure below, Product has been moved to the Column Labels and Customer has been added to the Row Labels.

Figure 129

Rearranging pivot table fields in Excel 2007

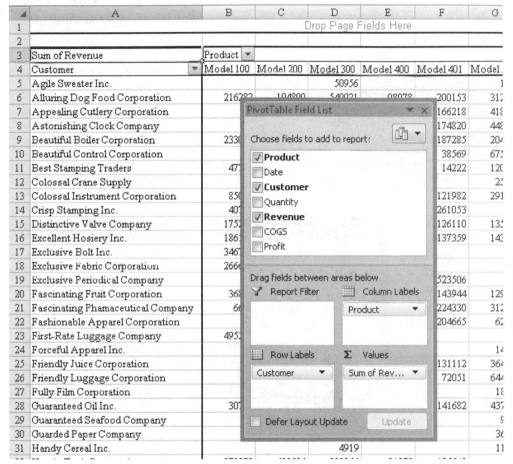

Eliminating Blank Cells from the Data Section

In the figure above, notice that Agile Sweater did not buy any of Model 100. Excel chooses to put a blank cell instead of a zero in this cell. If you have numeric data, blank cells are evil. You really want to have zeros instead of blanks.

The fix is somewhat buried. From the Excel 2003 PivotTable toolbar, choose the PivotTable dropdown and choose Table Options. In Excel 2007, use the Options icon in the PivotTable Options group of the PivotTable Tools Options ribbon.

1. In Excel 97-2003, on the right side of the PivotTable Options dialog, there is a setting "For empty cells show:". Type a zero in that box.

Analyzing w/ PivotTables

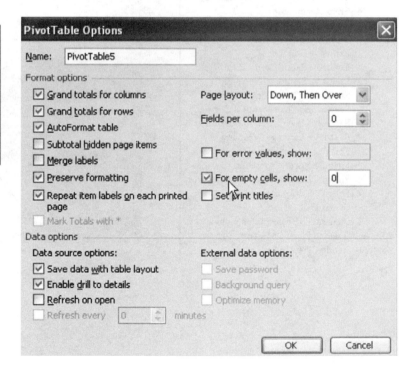

Figure 130

Using the PivotTable Options dialog to replace blank cells with zeros

In Excel 2007, use the Layout & Format tab of the PivotTable Options dialog. In the Format section, type a zero in the box "For Empty Cells, show:"

Figure 131

Using the Layout & format tab in Excel 2007 to replace empty cells with zeros

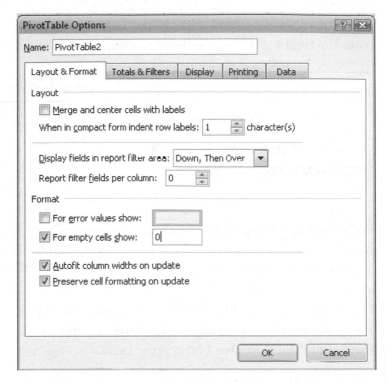

Changing a Pivot Table by Dragging Fields

Pivot Table veterans find it easiest to change the pivot table by simply dragging fields around the report.

This mode is automatically enabled in Excel 97-2003, but is hidden in Excel 2007. To enable it, use the Display tab of the PivotTable Options dialog. Choose the box for "Classic Pivot Table layout (enables dragging of fields in the grid)".

You can take the gray field names on a report and drag them to a new location. You can also take fields from the PivotTable Field List and drop them on the report.

The key to getting this right is to watch the mouse cursor and the gray squiggly insertion point.

Say that you want to add dates to the left side of the report. Drag the Date field from the field list and move it over column A.

	A	B
1		
2		
3	Sum of Revenue	Product ▼
4	Customer	▼ Model 100]
5	Agile Sweater Inc.	
6	Alluring Dog Food Corporation	216282
7	Appealing Cutlery Corporation	
8	Astonishing Clock Company	
9	Beautiful Boiler Corporation	233040
10	Beautiful Control Corporation	
11	Best Stamping Traders	47717
12	Colossal Crane Supply	
13	Colossal Instrument Corporation	85078

Figure 132

Blue shading in mouse cursor indicates field will be dropped in Row area of pivot table

While you are dragging the field, the mouse pointer changes to an outline of the pivot table. One of the four sections of the outline will be highlighted in blue. When your mouse is over column A, the Row area of the pivot table outline is highlighted in blue to indicate that you are about to drop the field in the Row area of the pivot table.

In the preceding figure, notice the gray squiggly line between columns A and B. This indicates that if you drop the field, you will see dates within each customer.

	A	B
2		
3	Sum of Revenue	
4	Customer	▼ Date ▼]
5	Agile Sweater Inc.	12/23/01
6		4/12/02
7		11/12/03
8		4/24/04
9	Agile Sweater Inc. Total	
10	Alluring Dog Food Corporation	4/9/97
11		5/3/97
12		5/8/97

Figure 133

Result if Date field is dropped in column A

2. Instead, if you drag the field to the left side of column A, the gray squiggly insertion point will be on the left side of column A (although it is barely visible in this book).

Figure 134

Note location of gray squiggly line to determine targeted drop area

2	
3	Sum of Revenu
4	Customer
5	Agile Sweater
6	All ⎯ng Dog F
7	Appe ☐g Cut
8	Astonishing C
9	Beautiful Boile

3. Dropping the field here will show customers within each date.

Figure 135

Showing customers within Date

1		
2		
3	Sum of Revenue	
4	Date ▼	Customer
5	1/1/96	First-Rate Luggage Company
6		Magnificent Hosiery Inc.
7		Savory Argon Company
8	1/1/96 Total	
9		1/2/96 Savory Argon Company
10	1/2/96 Total	
11		1/3/96 Handy Tank Corporation
12		Savory Argon Company
13	1/2/96 Total	

4. To remove a field, drag the field heading off the page until the mouse cursor changes to a red X.

Figure 136

Cursor indicates that you are removing a field by dragging it off the page

5. To move a field to the top row of the report, the mouse pointer will have the Column area of the toolbar highlighted.

Figure 137

Blue highlight in Column area of mouse pointer indicates that's where the field will be dropped

	A	B	C
1			
2			
3	Sum of Revenue	Product ▼	
4	Date ▼	Model 100	Mo 200
5	1/1/96	41407	4597
6	1/2/96	0	1403

Showing Two or More Fields in the Data Area

You can choose to show Quantity, Revenue, and Profit in the Data section of the pivot table.

1. Drag a new field and drop it in the middle of the table. The mouse pointer will highlight the Data area.

Figure 138 Data area is highlighted in the mouse pointer

2. Once you've added multiple data fields, you will have a new gray field called Data. You can drag this heading around to show the data items in various views. The default view is to show the three data fields as the innermost Row area item.

Analyzing w/ PivotTables

Figure 140

Default Data area view in Row area

	A	B	C	D
1				D
2				
3			Product ▾	
4	Date ▾	Data ▾	Model 100	Model 200 N
5	1/1/96	Sum of Revenue	41407	45970
6		Sum of Quantity	1958	2004
7		Sum of Profit	13349	14830
8	1/2/96	Sum of Revenue	0	14039
9		Sum of Quantity	0	598

Figure 139

Moving Data field to the Row area provides a better view

	A	B	C	D
1		Drop Page Fields Here		
2				
3		Data ▾		
4	Product ▾	Sum of Revenue	Sum of Quantity	Sum of Profit
5	Model 100	7185683	333361	2681109
6	Model 200	11742434	548838	4264271
7	Model 300	17503910	817766	6892334
8	Model 400	2365834	111460	731629
9	Model 401	5722595	267327	2210715
10	Model 500	11683397	550323	4313654
11	Model 600	7503486	350584	2624176
12	Model 700	1710952	79693	569802
13	Grand Total	65418291	3059352	24287690

3. It often makes more sense to move the Data field to the Column area.

Grouping Date Fields by Year

The data in this example is transactional data down to the daily level. You will usually want to spot trends by month or year. It is easy to group the transactional dates up to a year level.

1. Move the Date field as a field going down column A of the report. (With 10 years of data, there will not be room for the dates to go across the top of the report).

2. In Excel 97-2003: Right-click the Date field. Choose Group and Show Detail → Group.
   In Excel 2007: Select one date in the grid and then use PivotTable Tools Options → Group → Group Field.

Figure 141

Selecting Group and Show Detail from the Data field right-click menu

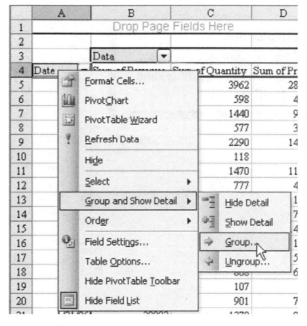

3. In the Grouping dialog, choose Years and unselect Months.

Figure 142

Changing Data field from months to years

Your Data field will now reflect years.

Figure 143

Pivot table showing sums of revenue, quantity, and profit by year

	A	B	C	D
1		Drop Page Fields Here		
2				
3		Data		
4	Date	Sum of Revenue	Sum of Quantity	Sum of Profit
5	1996	6264944	292794	2066444
6	1997	4709818	220105	1681366
7	1998	5588907	259001	2051946
8	1999	4665053	218555	1767228
9	2000	4837081	227504	1646789
10	2001	8212906	384871	3073868
11	2002	6061011	283166	2455101
12	2003	6636130	309649	2540745
13	2004	6936306	325240	2591398
14	2005	5695985	267202	2130630
15	2006	5810150	271265	2282175
16	Grand Total	65418291	3059352	24287690
17				

Grouping Date Fields by Month

This is not intuitive, but if you want data by month, you must group by month and year.

1. Try grouping by month, only. Notice that you get a poorly designed report that is useful only for seasonality analysis.

Figure 144

Data fields grouped by month only are virtually useless

(Cell B5 shows the total of each January from 1996 through 2006)

	A	B	C	D
1		Drop Page Fields Here		
2				
3		Data		
4	Date	Sum of Revenue	Sum of Quantity	Sum of Profit
5	Jan	5083632	238832	1866289
6	Feb	4773779	224272	1776199
7	Mar	5348827	248850	1985872
8	Apr	4788869	224543	1768825
9	May	5175961	241772	1934794
10	Jun	4950889	231315	1841828
11	Jul	5368540	252266	1992978
12	Aug	5642857	265473	2121519
13	Sep	5349302	248798	1968614
14	Oct	6363691	295944	2384791
15	Nov	6323059	294923	2334412
16	Dec	6248885	292364	2311569
17	Grand Total	65418291	3059352	24287690

Analyzing w/ PivotTables

2. Instead, choose to group by Month and Year. Now the Date field reflects months and a new field called Year is available.

Figure 145

Data fields grouped by month and year provide useful information

	A	B	C	
1			Drop Page Fields
2				
3			Data ▼	
4	Years ▼	Date ▼	Sum of Revenue	Sum
5	1996	Jan	543792	
6		Feb	457302	
7		Mar	392130	
8		Apr	400204	
9		May	410700	
10		Jun	476777	
11		Jul	492456	
12		Aug	542395	
13		Sep	750449	
14		Oct	703926	
15		Nov	645638	
16		Dec	449175	
17	1997	Jan	436829	
18		Feb	333304	
19		Mar	372658	

3. The fact that month and year are now two different fields allows you to build an interesting report with years going across the top and months down the side. Move the fields as shown in the following figure. This allows you to compare year vs. year results by month.

Analyzing w/ PivotTables

Figure 146

Comparing yearly results a month at a time

	A	B	C	D
1				
2				
3		Data ▼	Years ▼	
4		Sum of Revenue		
5	Date ▼	1996	1997	1998
6	Jan	543792	436829	355190
7	Feb	457302	333304	308366
8	Mar	392130	372658	533256
9	Apr	400204	405547	499009
10	May	410700	394613	267360
11	Jun	476777	271721	389425
12	Jul	492456	392247	361578
13	Aug	542395	338793	440566
14	Sep	750449	268504	497829
15	Oct	703926	524628	616258
16	Nov	645638	483528	645353
17	Dec	449175	487446	674717
18	Grand Total	6264944	4709818	5588907
19				

Removing One of Many Data Items

In the preceding figure, you may want to focus only on revenue.

In Excel 97-2003: To remove Quantity and Profit, use the dropdown on the Data field. You can now uncheck Quantity and Profit.
In Excel 2007: Simply uncheck Quantity and Profit from the top of the Pivot Table Field List.

Figure 147

Remove data items by selecting dropdown and unchecking the items

Building an Ad-Hoc Report Using Page Fields or Report Filter

There is a fourth area of a pivot table. In Excel 97-2003, it is called the Page area. In Excel 2007, it is called the Report Filter.

1. Move several fields to the Page area at the top of the report.

Figure 148

Moving fields to the Page area

	A	B	C	D
1	Product	(All)		
2	Customer	(All)		
3	Years	(All)		
4				
5		Data		
6		Sum of Quantity	Sum of Revenue	Sum of Profit
7	Total	3059352	65418291	24287690
8				
9				

2. There is now a drop-down for each field in the Page area.

   If you select the dropdown, you can query to find just the sales of Model 100 to Best Stamping or any other conceivable ad-hoc query.

Figure 149

Using a dropdown to make queries

	A	B	C	D
1	Product	Model 100 ▾		
2	Customer	Best Stamping Traders ▾		
3	Years	(All) ▾		
4				
5		Data ▾		
6		Sum of Revenue	Sum of Quantity	Sum of Profit
7	Total	47717	2342	17022

Showing Top 10 Customers

In the figure below, the customers are presented in alphabetical order.

Figure 150

Pivot table with Customer field in alphabetical order is of limited use

	A	B	C
1	Product	Model 100 ▾	
2	Years	(All) ▾	
3			
4	Sum of Revenue		
5	Customer ▾	Total	
6	Alluring Dog Food Corporation	216282	
7	Beautiful Boiler Corporation	233040	
8	Best Stamping Traders	47717	
9	Colossal Instrument Corporation	85078	
10	Crisp Stamping Inc.	40718	
11	Distinctive Valve Company	175234	
12	Excellent Hosiery Inc.	186122	
13	Exclusive Bolt Inc.	346722	

1. In Excel 97-2003, double-click the Customer field to get to the nearly useless PivotTable Field dialog. From this dialog, choose the Advanced button.

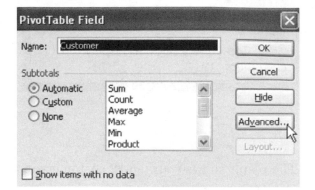

Figure 151

Select the Advanced button to make many useful options available

2. On the PivotTable Advanced Field Options dialog, you can control the sort order of the Customer field.

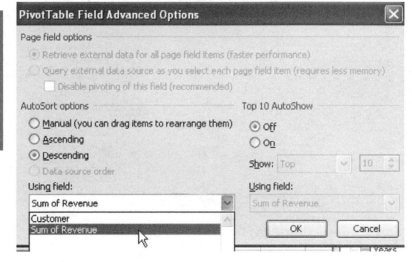

Figure 152

Sorting the Customer field in descending order based on sum of Revenue

3. You can also use the AutoShow option to show just the top or bottom 5, 10, or 20 items.

Figure 153

Using Top 10 AutoShow to display top 12 customers

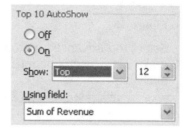

Top 10 AutoShow

○ Off
◉ On

Show: Top   ▾   12 ⬍

Using field:

Sum of Revenue   ▾

The result shows your top 12 customers in descending order based on revenue.

Figure 154

Resulting display has much more value than original alphabetical sort

	A	B
1	Product	Model 100 ▾
2		
3	Sum of Revenue	
4	**Customer** ▾	Total
5	Host Marriott Corp.	804931
6	Triad Hospitals Inc.	783685
7	ConAgra Foods Inc. Omaha	621557
8	The Williams Cos. Inc.	518796
9	Wal-Mart	495294
10	American International Group	457211
11	CIGNA Corp.	381480
12	Leggett & Platt	346722
13	TransMontaigne Inc.	321591
14	Constellation Energy Group Inc.	295840
15	Albertson's Inc.	270970
16	The Dow Chemical Co.	266668
17	Grand Total	5564745
18		

Sorting and Filtering is far easier in Excel 2007.

1. Hover over the Customer field in the **top** portion of the Pivot Table Field List. A new dropdown arrow appears as shown here.

Figure 155

Finding the Customer field dropdown arrow

2. When you select the dropdown, you have Sort options, and Filter options leading to a Top 10 filter as shown here.

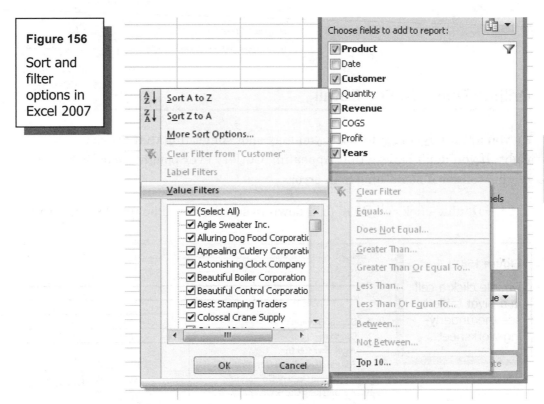

Figure 156

Sort and filter options in Excel 2007

3. Choose More Sort Options... to access the Sort (Customer) dialog.

Figure 157

Options in the Sort (Customer) dialog

Drilling Down To See Detail

As you are analyzing your data, you may spot something that doesn't look right. If you don't believe that Appealing Cutlery ever bought model 300, you might wonder if something is in error.

1. Double-click cell D9 to drill down to see the detail behind that figure.

Figure 158

Double click a cell in a pivot table to see the underlying worksheet

	A	B	C	D
1				
2				
3			Drop Page Fie
4				
5	Sum of Revenue	Product ▼		
6	Customer ▼	Model 100	Model 200	Model 300	M
7	Agile Sweater Inc.			50956
8	Alluring Dog Food Corporation	216282	194800	549921
9	Appealing Cutlery Corporation		13972	559214
10	Astonishing Clock Company		23611	294780
11	Beautiful Boiler Corporation	233040	205112	538239

You will be given a new worksheet with just the Model 300 records for Appealing Cutlery.

Figure 159

Underlying worksheet for the records

	A	B	C	D	E	F	G
1	**Product**	**Date**	**Customer**	**Quantity**	**Revenue**	**COGS**	**Profit**
2	Model 300	6/24/2000	Appealing Cutlery Corporation	528	10879	6755	4124
3	Model 300	8/24/2000	Appealing Cutlery Corporation	343	8077	5076	3001
4	Model 300	10/11/2000	Appealing Cutlery Corporation	866	18872	12523	6349
5	Model 300	10/13/2000	Appealing Cutlery Corporation	823	19709	12560	7149
6	Model 300	10/30/2000	Appealing Cutlery Corporation	905	21886	13487	8399

Pivot Tables and Recalculation

If you change values in the original source data, the pivot table does not automatically recalculate! This is because Excel copied your source data into memory in order to allow the pivot table to calculate very quickly.

1. To force Excel to re-read the source data and re-calc the pivot table, use the red exclamation point on the PivotTable Toolbar in Excel 97-2003 or the Refresh button on the PivotTable Tools Options ribbon in Excel 2007.

Analyzing w/ PivotTables

Figure 160

Selecting the Refresh Data button to refresh the pivot table data source and calculations in Excel 97-2003

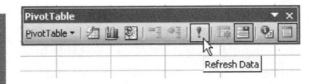

Figure 161

Selecting the Refresh button on the PivotTable Tools Options ribbon to refresh the pivot table data source and calculations in Excel 2007

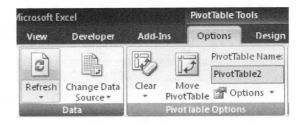

Limitations on Using Pivot Tables

While pivot tables are fantastic at summarizing data, they have a few strange limitations. You cannot insert rows or columns in the middle of a pivot table.

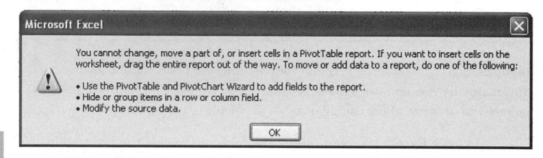

Figure 162

Use Paste Special – Values to reformat as desired

Analyzing w/
PivotTables

You may find it convenient to use the pivot table feature to create a summary and then to change the report to static values in order to reformat the summary for use in a PowerPoint presentation or some other use.

1. Select the entire pivot table, including the blank rows where the page fields might go. Copy the table to the clipboard with Ctrl+C.

2. Then, use Edit → Paste Special → Values to convert the table to values. In Excel 2007: Use Home → Paste → Paste Values. You can now reformat as needed.

Reporting Percentage of Row

So far, all of the examples have presented the Data field as a SUM of a field such as Revenue. There are many other options.

Figure 163

Accessing powerful pivot table options

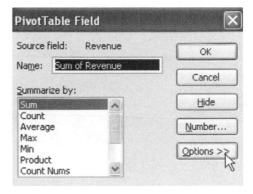

1. Double-click the Sum of Revenue field in A3 to access the PivotTable Field dialog for Revenue. While you can change from Sum to Count or Average here, the really powerful options are hidden behind the Options button in Excel 97-2003 or on the Show Values As tab in Excel 2007.

2. Choosing the Options button opens up additional choices where you can express the figures as percentages of the total, or other various items.

Figure 164

Using the "Show data as" option

3. The "Show data as" dropdown offers Normal and several other percentage options.

Figure 165

Selecting "% of row" option

Show data as:

Normal
Difference From
% Of
% Difference From
Running Total in
% of row
% of column
% of total

4. Select the "% of row" option. Each row adds up to 100%.

Figure 166 Selecting % of row option shows percentage of each product purchased by each customer totaling 100% of each customer's purchases

	A	B	C	D	E	F	G	H	I	J
1					Drop Page Fields Here					
2										
3	Sum of Revenue	Product								
4	Customer	Model 100	Model 200	Model 300	Model 400	Model 401	Model 500	Model 600	Model 700	Grand Total
5	Chevron	0.00%	0.00%	0.00%	0.00%	0.00%	35.80%	64.20%	0.00%	100.00%
6	Bell Canada	0.00%	0.00%	0.00%	0.00%	0.00%	65.96%	7.30%	26.74%	100.00%
7	Phillip Morris	0.00%	0.00%	22.57%	0.00%	0.00%	37.64%	39.80%	0.00%	100.00%
8	Kroger	0.00%	0.00%	96.49%	0.00%	0.00%	3.51%	0.00%	0.00%	100.00%
9	Gildan Activewear	0.00%	0.00%	0.00%	0.00%	0.00%	51.34%	48.66%	0.00%	100.00%
10	Compaq	0.00%	0.00%	66.53%	0.00%	0.00%	22.31%	11.17%	0.00%	100.00%
11	Sears	0.00%	0.00%	11.26%	0.00%	0.00%	25.33%	25.95%	37.46%	100.00%
12	Texaco	0.00%	0.00%	25.83%	0.00%	0.00%	39.19%	34.98%	0.00%	100.00%
13	Compton Petroleum	0.00%	0.00%	14.34%	0.00%	0.00%	33.37%	52.29%	0.00%	100.00%
14	Air Canada	0.00%	0.00%	56.43%	0.00%	0.00%	0.00%	16.15%	27.42%	100.00%
15	Grand Total	0.00%	0.00%	28.45%	0.00%	0.00%	32.85%	30.22%	8.48%	100.00%
16										

Analyzing w/
PivotTables

The following setting shows each year's revenue as a percentage of 1996 revenue.

Figure 167

Selecting a "Show data as" option other than the default of Normal enables the "Base field" and "Base item" options

This setting would show each year's revenue as a percentage of the previous year's revenue.

Figure 168

Experiment with these settings to discover the powerful ways they can help you interpret your data

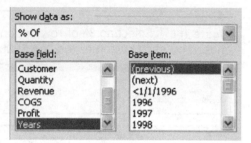

Analyzing Results by Date

Here's the Situation

You have a database of transactional records by date. You would like to see how many records happened on each date. Such an analysis might lead to more questions about spikes on a particular date, etc.

Here's What to Do

While a pivot table or data consolidation would give you a summary of all dates in the dataset, these methods would leave out dates that might be missing from the dataset.

A better approach would be to build a list of dates when you expect the transactions to appear. Then, use COUNTIF and SUMIF to analyze the records by date.

Analyzing by Date

Filling in Weekdays

The dataset contains a list of customer payments received during 2007. Your accounts payable department works Monday through Friday, excepting 10 holidays a year.

You would expect to find numerous checks received on every day of the year.

In a blank section of the worksheet, build a list of weekday dates by following these steps:

1. Enter 1/2/2007 in a cell. Press Ctrl+Enter to stay in that cell.

2. Right-click the fill handle. Drag down approximately 270 cells. The tool tip will be predicting a date in September. Ignore the tooltip.

3. When you release the mouse button, choose Fill Weekdays from the context menu as shown in Figure 169.

Figure 169

Fill Handle dropdown menu options

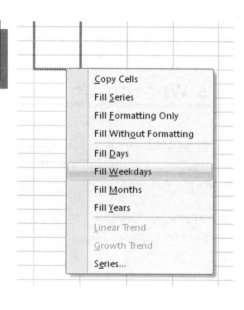

Analyzing by Date

4. If the column is not wide enough to handle dates in December, you will see ####### in those cells. Double-click the border between the F and G column letters as shown in Figure 170. This will extend column F to be as wide as the longest entry.

Figure 170

Cursor changes to crosshatch to indicate the border between two columns

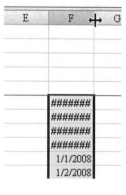

5. If your fill handle drag created dates in 2008, select those dates. Press the Delete key to clear those cells.

Filling in Conditional Counts

The next step is to count how many payments were processed on each day.
Follow these steps.

1. Enter the heading of Count in G5.

2. The syntax is =COUNTIF(Range,Criteria).
   In this case, the range is $C$6:$C$16831 and the criteria is the date
   from F6.
   In cell G6, type =COUNTIF(.

3. Press the Left Arrow key four times to move to C6. Press the End key.
   Press Shift+Down Arrow to highlight the range of dates. Press the F4
   key to add dollar signs to make the reference absolute.

4. Type a comma. Press the Left Arrow key to move to F6. Type the closing
   parentheses. Press Ctrl+Enter to accept the formula without moving to
   another cell.

5. Double-click the fill handle to copy the formula down to all dates.

As shown in Figure 171, you will now have the number of payments processed
for every day during the period.

Analyzing by Date

Figure 171

Column G contains the number of records per day

			G6	▼		f_x	=COUNTIF($C$6:$C$16831,F6)		

	B	C	D	E	F	G	H
1							
2	ıt Journal						
3	; ending December 31, 2007						
4							
5	Customer	Date	Amount		Date	Count	
6	Mighty Instrument Inc.	1/2/2007	2086.44		1/2/2007	78	
7	Sure Spring Traders	1/2/2007	1773.61		1/3/2007	120	
8	Supreme Bottle Supply	1/2/2007	2845.66		1/4/2007	76	
9	Persuasive Bolt Corporation	1/2/2007	3117.12		1/5/2007	87	
10	Honest Bottle Inc.	1/2/2007	3638.5		1/8/2007	124	
11	Paramount Machinery Company	1/2/2007	6202.29		1/9/2007	24	
12	Wonderful Door Partners	1/2/2007	4114.09		1/10/2007	71	
13	Ideal Curtain Corporation	1/2/2007	5009.36		1/11/2007	71	
14	Enhanced Telephone Inc.	1/2/2007	6910.78		1/12/2007	43	

Further Analysis – Sorting

Analyzing by Date

1. Sort the data by column G ascending.

    You would expect certain dates, such a company holidays, to have zero (0) transactions. If any other dates have zero transactions, they are worthy of investigation.

2. Remove the cells that have zero transactions and are holidays.

    To do this in any version of Excel, select the cells in both column F & G. Press Alt+E. Press Alt+D. In the Delete dialog, select Shift Cells Up. Click OK.

Further Analysis – Charting

It would be interesting to chart the data on a Line chart to see if the receipts are trending up, trending down, or have any pattern.

 Tip:

When either the row or column labels contain dates or numeric values, the top-left cell of the chart range should be blank. Before creating the chart, delete the value in F5.

1. Sort the data by column F ascending.

2. Select F5:G256.

3. In Excel 97-2003: Click the Chart Wizard button in the standard toolbar. Choose a Line chart and click Finish.
   In Excel 2007: Use the Insert ribbon. In the Chart group, click the dropdown for a Line chart and then choose the first 2-D line.

The resulting chart is shown in Figure 172.

Analyzing by Date

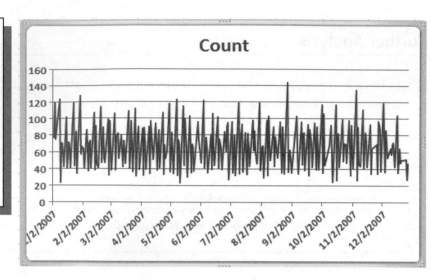

Figure 172

Chart showing the number of items received by accounts payable each workday

When you look at the chart, there are a few observations you can make:

- The receipts usually vary between 40 and 100 items each day.

- There are two days, one early in January, and one early in May, where there were barely 20 checks that came in.

- Near the beginning of October and the beginning of November, there were a few days where the checks were more than twice the normal rate.

- There appears to be neither an upward nor a downward trend in receipts.

- There is some unusual spikey behavior. There are plenty of spikes, but rarely are two adjacent days spiked. That seems unusual.

Analyzing by Date

Further Analysis – Stratification by Weekday

Add a heading in H5 called Weekday.

There are two formulas that you could use to convert a date to a weekday.

The WEEKDAY(F6) formula will convert a date to a number from 1 to 7. I can never remember that Monday=2 and Friday=6. Every time I use the WEEKDAY function, I have to do a little experiment to figure out the =WEEKDAY(TODAY()) to figure out how the function works.

Instead, use =TEXT(F6,"DDDD"). This converts the date in F6 to a day of the week that is spelled out.

1. Copy the TEXT formula down column H for all of the days of the year.

2. In J, build a list of the weekdays, from Monday through Friday.

My initial thought would be to use SUMIF to add up the receipts on each day of the week. However, because six of the ten holidays are Mondays, this might skew the numbers.

Analyzing by Date

3. If you are using Excel 2007, there is a brand new AVERAGEIF function and the formula in K9 would be:

    =AVERAGEIF($H$6:$H$256,J9,$G$6:$G$256)

    If you are using an older version of Excel, you would have to divide the SUMIF by COUNTIF formulas.

    =SUMIFIF($H$6:$H$256,J9,$G$6:$G$256)/
    COUNTIFIF($H$6:$H$256,J9)

4. Build a Column chart from this data.

Figure 173

Column chart built using the AVERAGEIF function

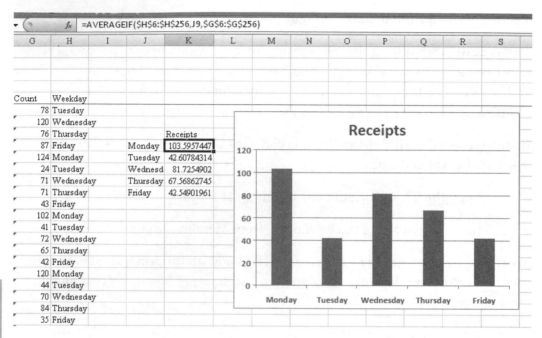

Analyzing by Date

When looking at the chart, Tuesday might make sense. No businesses mail checks on Saturday. Friday doesn't make sense. With mid-week check runs on Tuesday or Wednesday, you would think that Friday should be a busy day. You might find that all of the Friday afternoon checks are sitting in someone's desk drawer over the weekend.

Creating a Random Sample from a Dataset

Here's the Situation

You have 5000 rows of transaction data. You want to randomly audit 50 of the transactions.

Figure 174		
You have 5000 rows of data and need to select 50 for audit.		

	A	B	C
1	**Respondent**	**Date**	**Location**
2	TRUJILLO, SAMUEL	1-Jan-06	Desert Sky
3	RAYMOND, ROBIN	1-Jan-06	Deerbrook
4	ROBERTS, JASON	1-Jan-06	Deerbrook
5	GOFF, SHAWN	2-Jan-06	University Park
6	NIEVES, OPAL	2-Jan-06	Cottonwood
7	SNOW, JULIE	3-Jan-06	Cottonwood
8	FITZPATRICK, BETTY	4-Jan-06	Desert Sky
9	CERVANTES, BERTHA	5-Jan-06	Cottonwood
10	ROBERTS, MARLENE	5-Jan-06	Deerbrook
11	MENDOZA, SCOTT	5-Jan-06	Cottonwood

Random Samples

Here's What to Do

1. Create a new column heading called Random. In cell D2, enter the formula =RAND(). Re-select D2 and double-click the fill handle to copy this formula down to all rows.

This formula will assign each record a random decimal between 0 and 1.

Figure 175 Using RAND to generate a field of random numbers

=RAND()		
B	C	D
ate	**Location**	**Random**
1-Jan-06	Desert Sky	0.19047163
1-Jan-06	Deerbrook	0.71695289

2. Select cell D2 and press the AZ button in the Standard toolbar to sort. The first 100 customers in rows 2 through 101 are your random sample.

Figure 176

Using the AZ button to sort the customer data according to the random number field

	A	B	C	D
1	**Respondent**	**Date**	**Location**	**Random**
2	SHAFFER, SCOTT	10-Jul-06	Oakwood	0.17160266
3	FERRELL, STEPHEN	27-Apr-06	Fashion Valley	0.85736027
4	TURNER, EDWARD	26-Jan-06	Fashion Valley	0.63142938
5	ALVARADO, NORMAN	30-Apr-06	Cottonwood	0.87708004
6	ROBBINS, JO	29-Oct-06	Desert Sky	0.44451202
7	PICKETT, KIMBERLY	11-Oct-06	South Park	0.70297224
8	EWING, TINA	5-Apr-06	Deerbrook	0.56324993

Gotcha

Random Samples

In column D above, notice that these first 100 customers do not appear to have low numbers. That is because Excel recalculates the RAND function after you have sorted the data.

Finding and Analyzing Records Using AutoFilter

If you're doing any kind of data analysis, you might want to filter your responses so that you can see certain categories of records. Before I understood AutoFilter, I was killing myself doing sorts and inserting rows and calculating sums. It was frustrating, time consuming, and just plain ridiculous.

AutoFilter is a function that will make it easy for you to go through reams of data and get a fairly quick understanding of what's going on.

Here's the Situation

You have thousands of records to wade through.

Figure 177 Worksheet filled with records you need to sort

Analyzing w/ AutoFilter

	A	B	C	D	E	F	G	H
1	**Region**	**Product**	**Date**	**Customer**	**Quantity**	**Revenue**	**COGS**	**Profit**
2	Central	DEF	12/31/06	Tenet Healthcar	1126	23473	11083	12390
3	Central	ABC	12/31/06	Tenet Healthcar	102	1863	868	995
4	Central	XYZ	12/31/06	VF Corp.	318	7060	3250	3810
5	Central	XYZ	12/31/06	Monsanto Co.	1010	24682	10325	14357
6	Central	ABC	12/31/06	Cardinal Health	479	8602	4059	4543
7	Central	DEF	12/31/06	Computer Scier	699	15031	6885	8146
8	East	DEF	12/31/06	Medco Health S	239	5671	2353	3318

Here's What to Do

Use the AutoFilter command to find certain records. The AutoFilter feature can be toggled on or off using Data → Filter → AutoFilter in Excel 97-2003 or using Data → Filter in Excel 2007. When the feature is turned on, a dropdown appears on each heading.

Figure 178 Using AutoFilter

	A	B	C	D	E	F	G	H
1	Region ▼	Produc ▼	Da ▼	Customer ▼	Quant ▼	Reven ▼	CO(▼	Pr(▼
2	Central	DEF	12/31/06	Tenet Healthcar	1126	23473	11083	12390
3	Central	ABC	12/31/06	Tenet Healthcar	102	1863	868	995

1. Turn on the AutoFilter feature.

2. To find all East sales of product ABC, select East from the Region dropdown and ABC from the Product dropdown.

Analyzing w/ AutoFilter

Figure 179

Using AutoFilter to find all the East sales sorted alphabetically by Product

	A	B	
1	Region ▼	Produc ▼	
8	Ea	Sort Ascending	12
9	Ea	Sort Descending	12
10	Ea	(All)	12
15	Ea	(Top 10...)	12
22	Ea	(Custom...)	12
24	Ea	ABC	12
25	Ea	DEF	12
	Ea	XYZ	

You will now only see the desired records. The dropdown arrow for these two columns changes from black to blue. The row numbers for the visible rows change to blue to indicate that a filter is applied.

Figure 180 Blue dropdown arrows indicate filtered fields

	A	B	C	D	E	F	G	H
1	Region ▼	Produc ▼	Da ▼	Customer ▼	Quant ▼	Reven ▼	CO(▼	Pr(▼
9	East	ABC	12/31/06	CSX	1030	19229	8728	10501
10	East	ABC	12/31/06	Lear Corp.	712	13370	6033	7337
22	East	ABC	12/30/06	Constellation Er	322	5868	2732	3136
26	East	ABC	12/30/06	Boise Cascade	525	10117	4446	5671
30	East	ABC	12/30/06	Caesars Enterta	521	10051	4418	5633
33	East	ABC	12/30/06	Boise Cascade	795	14990	6735	8255

Excel Details

Copying Only Filtered Records

To copy these records, you have to select Visible Cells Only. This is an obscure option found through the Go To dialog.

1. First, select the entire range of cells, from A1 down through H of the last row.
    Using Ctrl+* will select the current region.

2. Press Ctrl+; to select the visible cells only.

It is barely noticeable, but Excel will add thin gray bands in the selection area to indicate that the hidden rows are not part of the selection.

Figure 181

Thin gray bands indicate where there are hidden rows that will not be included in the copy and paste

	A	B	C
1	Region ▼	Produc ▼	Da ▼
9	East	ABC	12/31/06
10	East	ABC	12/31/06
22	East	ABC	12/30/06
26	East	ABC	12/30/06

3. Once you have selected the visible cells, you can copy and paste the matching records to a new worksheet.

Analyzing w/ AutoFilter

4. To show all records again, you can reset all headings with filters back to (All) or select Data → Filter → Show All in Excel 97-2003 or Data → Sort & Filter → Clear in Excel 2007.

Still More AutoFilter Options

AutoFilter offers some other cool options.

1. Choose (Top 10...) from the Revenue dropdown to display this dialog. Choose to show the top 10% of records as shown below.

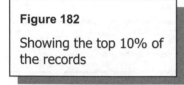

Figure 182

Showing the top 10% of the records

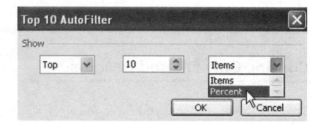

2. Select (Custom...) from the Date dropdown. You can build a criteria to get a range of dates.

Figure 183

Using the Custom filter dialog to obtain a selected range of dates

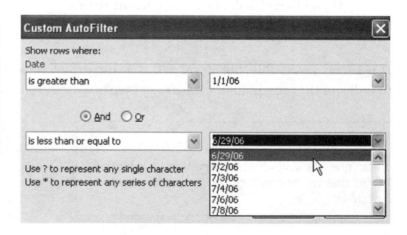

Formula Auditing

Here's the Situation

You have received a new spreadsheet. One of the first things that you will want to do is to find all of the cells that contain formulas. Once you've identified the formulas, you can use Excel's auditing tools to understand them.

Here's What to Do

Locating All Formulas with Show Formulas Mode

When you inherit a spreadsheet from someone else, it is good to figure out which cells are input values and which cells are formulas.

When you look at the spreadsheet in Figure 184, it is hard to figure out which cells are formulas and which are values.

Figure 184 Someone built this spreadsheet. Which cells contain formulas?

	G4	▾		*fx*	=3*12*30*6				

▲	A	B	C	D	E	F	G	H	I	J
1	Section 1: Historical Trends (Per Month)									
2										
3		Store Type	Size	Rent	Sales	Profit	Labor	Net		
4		Regular	1200	2400	12456	6228	6480	-2652		
5		BigBox	2600	5200	34500	17250	8640	3410		
6										
7	Section 2: Number of Stores									
8										
9		Regular	81							
10		BigBox	184							
11										
12	Section 3: Analysis of Profitability of Current Store Mix									
13			Sales	Net Profit	NP%					
14		Total Chain	88283232	4951536	5.6%					
15		Regular	12107232	-2577744	-21.3%					
16		Big Box	76176000	7529280	9.9%					
17										
18	Section 4: Profit Projections with a New Mix of Stores									
19				Sales	Profit	NP%				
20		Regular	0	0	0					
21		BigBox	240	99360000	9820800					
22		New Mix	240	99360000	9820800	10%				
23										
24	Cost of Closing Stores									
25		Labor	787320							
26		Lost Rent	388800							
27					Year 1	Year 2	Year 3	Year 4	Year 5	Total
28	Increased Profit from New Stores				4869264	4869264	4869264	4869264	4869264	
29	Costs in year 1				1176120	0	0	0	0	
30	Bottom Line				3693144	4869264	4869264	4869264	4869264	23170200
31										
32			Big Formula	3980883						

There is a quick and easy way to display all of the formulas on the worksheet.

On American keyboards, in the upper left corner, there is a key with both a tilde (~) and a grave accent (`). The grave accent is a backwards apostrophe that looks like some accent marks used in other languages. The key is located below the Esc key, and to the left of the 1 key along the top of the keyboard.

This key is the secret for entering Show Formulas mode. Hold down Ctrl+` and Excel will show you the formula instead of the value in each cell as shown in Figure 185.

Figure 185 Which cells contain formulas? Press Ctrl+` to display formulas, not values.

| D32 | fx | =(E30/C4)^(D4/D5)+D14-E21*E16+Sheet2!C5 |

	A	B	C	D	E	F
1	Sect					
2						
3		Store Type	Size	Rent	Sales	Prof
4		Regular	1200	2400	12456	=+E4/2
5		BigBox	2600	=+C5*2	34500	=+E5/2
6						
7	Sect					
8						
9		Regular	81			
10		BigBox	184			
11						
12	Sect					
13			Sales	Net Profit	NP%	
14		Total Chain	=+C15+C16	=+D15+D16	=+D14/C14	
15		Regular	=(C9*E4)*12	=(C9*H4)*12	=+D15/C15	
16		Big Box	=(C10*E5)*12	=(C10*H5)*12	=+D16/C16	
17						
18	Sect					
19				Sales	Profit	NP%
20		Regular	0	=+C20*E4	=+C20*H4	
21		BigBox	240	=C21*E5*12	=+C21*H5*12	
22		New Mix	=SUM(C20:C21)	=SUM(D20:D21)	=SUM(E20:E21)	=+E22/D22
23						
24	Cos					
25		Labor	787320			
26		Lost Rent	=($C$9-$C$20)*D4*2			
27					Year 1	Year
28	Incr				=+E22-D14	=+E28
29	Cos				=+C26+C25	0
30	Bott				=+E28-E29	=+F28-F29
31						
32				Big Formula	=(E30/C4)^(D4/D5)+	
33						
34						
35						
36						
37						
38						
39						

Formula Auditing

Excel makes the columns a bit wider in Show Formulas mode. This helps with formulas like those in E22, but will not be wide enough to accommodate very long formulas like the one in D32.

When you select a cell in Show Formula mode, all of the precedent cells are surrounded by a border. The color of each border matches the color of the cell reference in the selected cell.

To exit Show Formulas mode, press Ctrl+` again.

This keyboard shortcut is very powerful for locating formulas and is an important tool in finding formula errors.

If you forget the keyboard shortcut, you can get to Show Formulas mode by one of these methods:

> ➢ In Excel 2007: Use the Formulas ribbon. In the Formula Auditing group, click Show Formulas.

> ➢ In Excel 97-2003: Use Tools → Formula Auditing → Formula Auditing Mode.

Highlighting All Formulas with Go To Special

Formula Auditing

Show Formulas mode is fine, but sometimes you might want something a bit more permanent to mark your formula cells. Using an obscure dialog box, it is easy to select all of the formula cells in a worksheet.

 Tip:

Select a single cell before the following steps. If you select a single cell, Excel will find all of the formulas in the entire worksheet. If you attempt the following steps with a range of cells selected, Excel will only find the formulas in the selected range. While this is also useful in certain situations, select a single cell for this example.

To display the Go To Special dialog box, follow one of these steps:

> ➢ In Excel 97-2003: Choose Edit → Go To. In the Go To dialog, click the Special button in the lower left corner.

> ➢ In Excel 2007: Display the Home ribbon. Near the right, in the Editing tab, click the dropdown for Find & Select. Choose Go To Special from the dropdown.

> ➢ In any version of Excel: Press the F5 key, followed by Alt+S.

> ➢ In any version of Excel: Press Alt+E, Alt+G, Alt+S.

As shown in Figure 186, the Go To Special dialog offers many powerful selection criteria. In this example, you want to select the option button for Formulas. If desired, you could limit the selection to only formulas that result in numbers, text, logicals, or errors.

Figure 186

Choose Formulas from the Go To Special dialog

With all of the checkboxes ticked, all of the formulas will be selected.

Formula Auditing

 Caution!

As this book goes to press, Excel 2007 is in the public beta. In both the Windows XP (blue) and Windows Vista (grey) color schemes, the color used to indicate a selection is extremely faint. We can hope this improves in the final release, but the odds seem slim. If it is not fixed by the release, then the 10% grey used to mark the highlighted cells is very difficult to see.

To permanently mark the selected cells, use the Fill Color dropdown to apply a fill color to the selected formula cells. The icon contains a paint bucket. It is found on the Formatting toolbar in Excel 97-2003 and in the Font group of the Home ribbon in Excel 2007. The Fill Color dropdown for Excel 2007 is shown in Figure 187. (Note how Excel 2007 offers a live preview of the cell color just by hovering over the color in the dropdown!)

Figure 187

Use the Fill Color dropdown to permanently color the formula cells

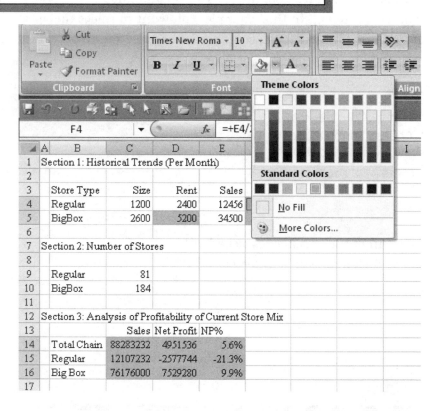

Formula Auditing

 Tip:

When many cells are selected, pressing the Enter key will move the active cell from cell to cell within the selection. This allows you to see the formula for each cell in the formula bar.

Evaluating a Formula with the F9 Key

Figure 189 shows a long formula in the formula bar. One portion of the formula has been selected by dragging the mouse.

Figure 188 Select one portion of a formula in the Formula bar

=(E30/C4)^(D4/D5)+D14-E21*E16+Sheet2!C5

When you press the F9 key, Excel will evaluate that portion of the formula and replace the references with the current value as shown in Figure 189.

Figure 189 Press F9 to evaluate the highlighted portion of the formula

=(E30/C4)^(0.461538461538462)+D14-E21*E16+Sheet2!C5

 Caution!

Be sure to press Esc to return the original terms to the formula.

To evaluate the whole formula, click into the formula bar and press F9 without selecting any characters.

Formula Auditing

Evaluating a Formula in Slow Motion

Excel 2003 offered a fantastic new feature called Evaluate Formula. In this mode, Excel will evaluate a formula in slow motion, step by step.

1. Select a cell that contains a formula.
   In Excel 2007: Use Formulas → Formula Auditing → Evaluate Formula.
   In Excel 2003: Use Tools → Formula Auditing → Evaluate Formula.

Figure 190 shows the Evaluate Formula dialog. E30 is underlined in the Evaluation box. This means that E30 is the first reference to be evaluated in the formula.

Figure 190 E30 will be the first term to be evaluated

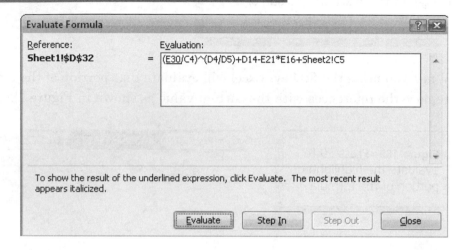

If you click Evaluate, Excel will replace E30 with the value in E30. C4 will become underlined to show that it is the next item to be calculated as shown in Figure 191.

Figure 191

Click Evaluate to convert the underlined reference to a value

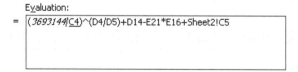

You can continue clicking Evaluate to solve the formula one step at a time. In the current example, it requires 17 steps to completely resolve the formula. After finishing the formula, you can either click Close or Restart.

Caution!

The Restart button only appears after completely evaluating the formula. If you need to restart in the middle, you have to click Close and then Evaluate Formula again.

Instead of clicking Evaluate for an underlined term, you can click Step In. This will open up a second evaluation frame, showing you that E30 is really comprised of E28+E29 as shown in Figure 192. You can either choose to evaluate E28, or Step In again. Click Step Out to close the lower evaluation frame and return to the prior evaluation frame.

Figure 192 Step In allows you to see the formula in a precedent cell

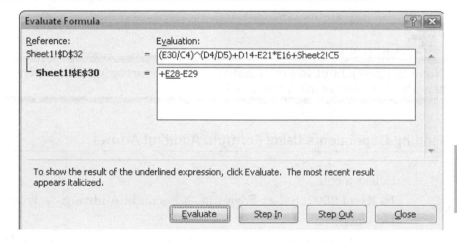

Formula Auditing

Tracing Precedents or Dependents

In the world of cell relationships, there are two important terms.

All of the cells that depend on the current cell are called dependents of that cell. A direct dependent is a cell that explicitly refers to the cell in its formula. There might be other cells that are dependent on the cell. The list of all dependents will include the cells dependent on a cell's direct dependents, the cells dependent on those cells, and so on.

A formula usually refers to other cells in order to calculate a result. The cells referenced in a formula are known as direct precedents. If you find the precedents of the direct precedent cells, and the precedents from those cells, and so on, you will eventually find the complete set of precedents located on the worksheet.

 Caution!

None of Excel's built-in functionality will locate precedents or dependents found on other worksheets in other workbooks.

Finding Dependents Using Formula Auditing Arrows

1. Select a cell.
   In Excel 2007: Select Formula → Formula Auditing → Trace Dependents.
   In Excel 97-2003: Use Tools → Formula Auditing → Trace Dependents.

In Figure 193, the Trace Dependents command was run on the 2600 square foot size in C5. Initially, Excel drew an arrow to indicate that the Rent in D5 was dependent on C5. While at first glance it may look like C5 is not all that important, remember that this is only the first-level dependent.

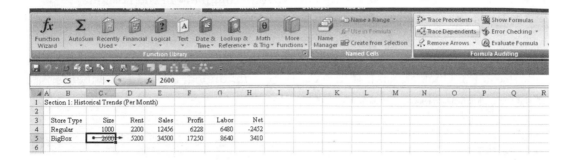

Figure 193 Don't be fooled; more than D5 is dependent on C5

2. With the first arrow drawn, click the Trace Dependents command again. You will see that H5 and D32 are also dependent on this cell.

Figure 194

After 11 clicks of the Trace Dependents icon, you will see that many cells are dependent on C5

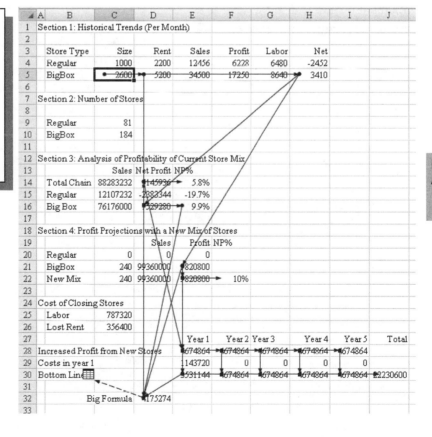

Note:

To remove the arrows, choose the Remove Arrows command in the Formula Auditing menu.

A faster way to find all dependents is to use the Go To Special dialog. Select a cell. Press F5. Click Special. In the Go To Special dialog, choose Dependents, and then All Levels as shown in Figure 195.

Figure 195

Select "All levels" of dependents to highlight all of the dependents in one step without having to click on Trace Dependents multiple times

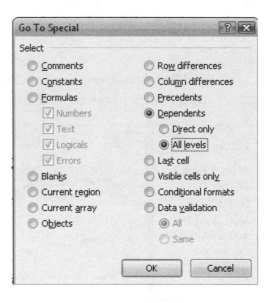

**Formula
Auditing**

Finding Precedents Using Formula Auditing Arrows

To find the cells used to calculate a formula, select the cell containing the formula, and then choose Trace Precedents. Excel will draw in arrows showing the direct dependents used to calculate the cell. In Figure 196, seven cells on the current worksheet are used to calculate cell D32. The icon at B30 means that additional precedent cells are on other worksheets.

Figure 196

The arrows show the first level precedents

Note:

Unfortunately, there is not a good way to figure out on which worksheets there are precedents. I sell an add-in to overcome this problem at http://www.mrexcel.com/traceprecedents.shtml.

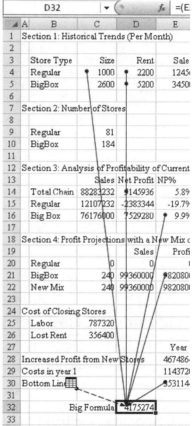

As in the previous example, if you continue clicking Trace Precedents, you will see that far more cells are used in the calculation of this value. Figure 197 shows all of the precedent cells.

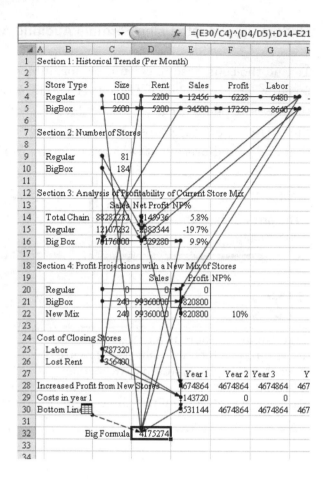

Figure 197

Click Trace Dependents multiple times to find all of the precedent cells

Formula Auditing Tips

There are a few common formula pitfalls. As you start to look at a spreadsheet, watch out for these problems.

Numeric Headings Included in AutoSum Totals

Figure 198 shows a simple enough worksheet. It has units for several regions for several years. Select cells B5:E5 and click the AutoSum button.

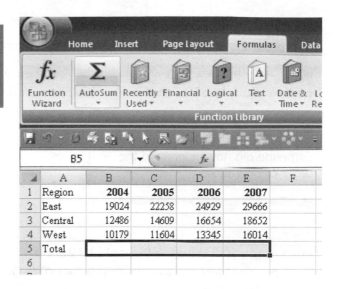

Figure 198

What will happen when you click the AutoSum?

Excel adds the totals, but includes the numeric headings in row 1 in the formula!

Figure 199

Numeric values of the headings included in the AutoSum

	A	B	C	D	E	F
1	Region	2004	2005	2006	2007	
2	East	19024	22258	24929	29666	
3	Central	12486	14609	16654	18652	
4	West	10179	11604	13345	16014	
5	Total	43693	50476	56934	66339	
6						

E5 · *fx* =SUM(E1:E4)

Formula Auditing

The IntelliSense used to enter the AutoSum formula can lead to a common worksheet error.

Ignoring Order of Operations

Figure 200 shows a very simple worksheet. Someone tried to average values from two samples. Unfortunately, this formula provided the wrong result.

Figure 200

Someone did not understand the order of operations

	D3		▼	f_x	=D1+D2/2

◢	A	B	C	D	E
1			Sample 1	200	
2			Sample 2	250	
3			Average	325	
4					

The average of 200 and 250 should be 225. If you are reading this book, you know that the proper formula should be =(D1+D2)/2. Or, even better, you could use =AVERAGE(D1:D2).

However, many novice Excellers assume that Excel will calculate the formula left to right. They assume that Excel would add D1+D2 first and then divide by 2. They assume incorrectly.

Just as a review, Excel evaluates a formula in this manner:

➢ First, any unary minus operators.

➢ Next, exponents using the ^ sign.

➢ Next, multiplication and division, left to right.

➢ Finally, addition and subtraction, left to right.

If you want to override the default order of operations, parentheses are in order.

You are allowed to nest parentheses. In math class you would have written {1+[4*5+(4-1)*2]/4}. In Excel, you simply stack up regular parentheses: (1+(4*5+(4-1)*2)/4).

Beware of Reset Error Indicators

If you enter an inconsistent error in Excel, the cell will be marked with a green triangle. A dropdown caution sign appears, alerting you to a possible problem with the formula, as shown in Figure 201.

Figure 201

This error icon alerts you that there might be a problem with the formula

51	69289.11	66571.89
70	3! ⚠ ▾	8680.89
71	37266.21	35804.79
11	46415.	The formula in this cell differs from the formulas in this area of the spreadsheet.
27	59224.77	56902.23

As shown in Figure 202, it is possible for someone to use the dropdown to Ignore the Error. This will cause the green indicator to disappear!

Figure 202

An analyst with a neatness obsession might clear the error markers

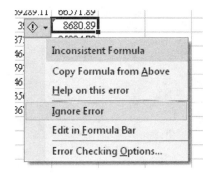

As an auditor, you can restore the error markers in the worksheet. The Error Checking Options has a button to Reset Ignored Errors. To access the Error Checking Options in a worksheet that has no error indicators, follow the appropriate steps:

> ➢ In Excel 97-2003: Use Tools → Error Checking and then click the Options button. In the Options dialog, click Reset Ignored Errors.

> ➢ In Excel 2007: Choose the Office icon menu, then Excel Options. Choose the Formulas category. In the Error Checking section, click Reset Ignored Errors as shown in Figure 203.

Figure 203

Reset the ignored errors before running an Error Check

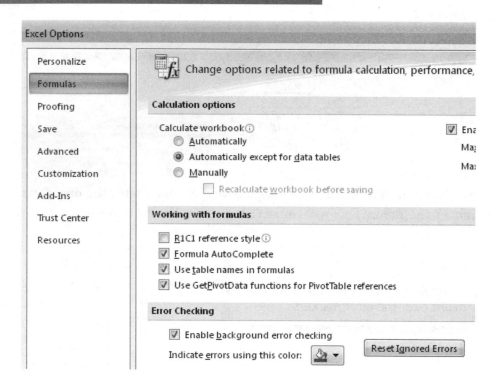

 Tip:

The error checking indicators are sometimes hard to notice. If you select the Error Checking command, you can step through the errors one at a time, as shown in Figure 204.

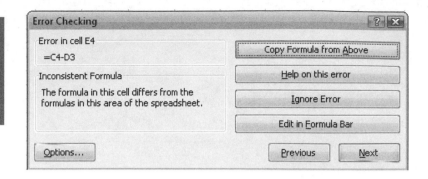

Figure 204

This dialog will show you the errors one at a time

**Formula
Auditing**

Matching Two Lists

Here's the Situation

Your company asks every employee to sign an ethics statement annually. You have one workbook with a list of all employees. You have a second workbook with a list of who has turned in their ethics statements.

You would like to find out which employees have not yet turned in their ethics statements.

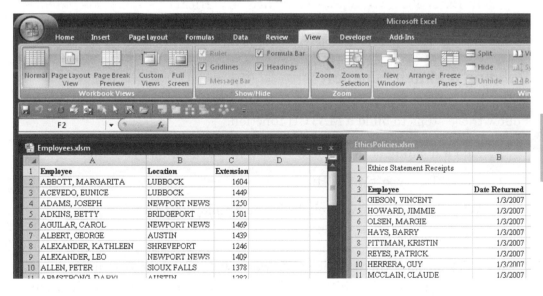

Figure 205

This figure shows the two workbooks

Here's What to Do

Assuming that both files have a field in common, you can use either VLOOKUP or MATCH. Ideally, you will have an employee number in both files; however, realistically, you will probably have to live with employee names.

Many people use VLOOKUP to return information from one table, but the MATCH function is a bit faster and can test if one value is located in another column.

Viewing Two Files Side-by-Side

It helps if you can see both files at the same time.

1. Open Excel and open the two files.

2. In Excel 97-2003: Use Window → Arrange → Vertical.
   In Excel 2007: Use View → Arrange → Vertical.

This will allow you to see both files side-by-side, as shown in Figure 205.

Building a Match Function

Follow these steps to build a MATCH function.

1. Add a heading of "Returned?" in cell D1 of the Employees file.

2. In cell D2, type =MATCH(

3. With the mouse, touch cell A2 in the Employees file.

4. Type a comma.

5. Click on the EthicsPolicies.xlsm window. Click in the first name in cell A4. Hold down the Shift key while pressing the End key and then the Down Arrow key. This selects the entire range of employee names. At this point, your formula in progress will be as follows:
   =MATCH(A2,[EthicsPolicies.xlsm]Sheet1!$A$4:$A$439

Note that Excel automatically puts in the dollar signs to make the second argument absolute because the range is located in another file.

6. Type a comma.

7. In Excel 2007, the AutoComplete tooltip will show you that the appropriate choice for an exact match is the value zero (0), as shown in Figure 206. Type 0 and a closing parenthesis.

Figure 206 AutoComplete tooltip can help you with proper syntax

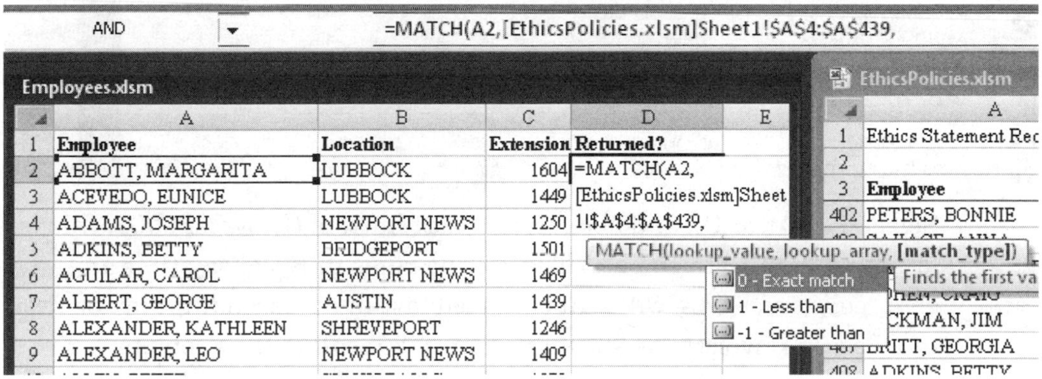

8. Press Enter to complete the formula. The answer will be either a number or the value #N/A. A number means that the employee was found in the other file, and therefore has returned his or her ethics statement.

9. Re-select cell D2. Double click the fill handle to copy the formula down to all employees. Any employees who do not have a signed ethics agreement will show up with a #N/A error value next to their names as shown in Figure 207.

Matching Two Lists

Figure 207

#N/A errors indicate employees who have not signed their ethics agreements

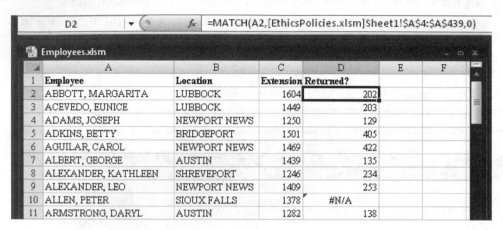

| D2 | | | f_x =MATCH(A2,[EthicsPolicies.xlsm]Sheet1!$A$4:$A$439,0) | | |

Employees.xlsm

	A	B	C	D	E	F
1	Employee	Location	Extension	Returned?		
2	ABBOTT, MARGARITA	LUBBOCK	1604	202		
3	ACEVEDO, EUNICE	LUBBOCK	1449	203		
4	ADAMS, JOSEPH	NEWPORT NEWS	1250	129		
5	ADKINS, BETTY	BRIDGEPORT	1501	405		
6	AGUILAR, CAROL	NEWPORT NEWS	1469	422		
7	ALBERT, GEORGE	AUSTIN	1439	135		
8	ALEXANDER, KATHLEEN	SHREVEPORT	1246	234		
9	ALEXANDER, LEO	NEWPORT NEWS	1409	253		
10	ALLEN, PETER	SIOUX FALLS	1378	#N/A		
11	ARMSTRONG, DARYL	AUSTIN	1282	138		

10. Select cell D1 or D2 and click the ZA sort button. (In Excel 2007, this is located on the Data ribbon.) The sorting rules in Excel say that any error cells, such as #N/A, will be sorted last in an ascending sort or first in a descending sort. As shown in Figure 208, all of the problem employees will appear at the top of the list.

Figure 208

#N/A errors cause problem employees to sort to the top of the list

Employees.xlsm

	A	B	C	D
1	Employee	Location	Extension	Returned?
2	ALLEN, PETER	SIOUX FALLS	1378	#N/A
3	BARRY, DARREN	NEWPORT NEWS	1695	#N/A
4	BELL, RAFAEL	AUSTIN	1618	#N/A
5	BISHOP, ETHEL	LUBBOCK	1532	#N/A
6	BOWEN, LONNIE	NEWPORT NEWS	1434	#N/A
7	BURT, KAY	NEWPORT NEWS	1203	#N/A
8	CAIN, VIOLA	LUBBOCK	1358	#N/A
9	CARLSON, WESLEY	BRIDGEPORT	1500	#N/A
10	CASE, FLOYD	SHREVEPORT	1658	#N/A
11	COMPTON, RUSSELL	NEWPORT NEWS	1448	#N/A
12	CONRAD, LOIS	SHREVEPORT	1694	#N/A
13	COPELAND, FLORENCE	NEWPORT NEWS	1207	#N/A

Allowing for More Names to Be Added

In theory, someone will keep adding new employees to the EthicsPolicies.xlsm file. To allow for this, edit the formula in D2 to include several hundred extra rows. This way, as new names are added to the second file, the formula will pick them up.

In Figure 207, edit the formula from:

=MATCH(A2,[EthicsPolicies.xlsm]Sheet1!$A$4:$A$439,0)

to

=MATCH(A2,[EthicsPolicies.xlsm]Sheet1!$A$4:$A$639,0)

Preventing #N/A Errors

The result of the MATCH function is a number. This number is actually the relative position of the employee in the lookup range. This is a rather meaningless answer.

Besides, some people may not want #N/A errors in their spreadsheet.

You can expand the formula using the =ISNA function. This function will test to see if the result of the function results in an #N/A error. If the result is an error, the ISNA function returns TRUE.

1. Change the heading in D1 to say "Missing?"

2. Change the formula to:

    =ISNA(MATCH(A2,[EthicsPolicies.xlsm]Sheet1!$A$4:$A$639,0))

3. Excel will display TRUE when the employee is missing from the other list, or FALSE when the employee is in the other list.

Note:

In addition to ISNA, Excel offers ISERROR and ISERR. The ISERROR function will return TRUE if the value is #N/A, #VALUE!, #REF!, #DIV/0!. #NUM!, #NAME?, or #NULL. The ISERR function checks for all of those errors except for the #N/A error.

The result of the new formula is shown in Figure 209.

Figure 209   #N/A error messages replaced with FALSE value

	A	B	C	D	E	F	G
	D2	fx =ISNA(MATCH(A2,[EthicsPolicies.xlsm]Sheet1!$A$4:$A$639,0))					
	Employees.xlsm						
1	**Employee**	**Location**	**Extension**	**Missing?**			
2	ABBOTT, MARGARITA	LUBBOCK	1604	FALSE			
3	ACEVEDO, EUNICE	LUBBOCK	1449	FALSE			
4	ADAMS, JOSEPH	NEWPORT NEWS	1250	FALSE			
5	ADKINS, BETTY	BRIDGEPORT	1501	FALSE			
6	AGUILAR, CAROL	NEWPORT NEWS	1469	FALSE			
7	ALBERT, GEORGE	AUSTIN	1439	FALSE			
8	ALEXANDER, KATHLEEN	SHREVEPORT	1246	FALSE			
9	ALEXANDER, LEO	NEWPORT NEWS	1409	FALSE			
10	ALLEN, PETER	SIOUX FALLS	1378	TRUE			

If you would rather use words instead of the TRUE/FALSE values, modify the formula to use the IF function.

=IF(ISNA(MATCH(A2,[EthicsPolicies.xlsm]Sheet1!$A$4:$A$639,0)),"Missing","OK")

This formula will return either the text "Missing" or the text "OK".

Retrieving the Date Returned Using VLOOKUP

The MATCH and VLOOKUP formulas both attempt to find a certain value in another range of values. When the MATCH function finds a value, it simply tells you the relative position of the match. The VLOOKUP function goes one step further and returns a value from a cell next to the match.

In the MATCH function, the second argument is a single column of data; A4:A639. With the VLOOKUP function, you would usually extend this range to include several columns of data. The EthicsPolicies.xlsm file contains two columns: Employee in column in A and Date Returned in column B.

There is a new third argument in VLOOKUP. This argument tells which column in the lookup range contains the value to return. This is a relative column number. If the lookup range were in J1:Z100, then column K would be the second column, and the third argument would be a 2. In this case, the value to be returned is in the second column of A2:B639, so the third argument is 2.

The fourth argument in VLOOKUP should be a FALSE, to indicate that you require an exact match. However, in the language of Excel, a zero is equivalent to FALSE. Thus, if you are editing the MATCH formula to be a VLOOKUP formula, it is fine to leave the fourth argument as a zero.

To change the original MATCH function to a VLOOKUP, follow these steps.

1. Edit the formula in D2. Change it to:

   =VLOOKUP(A2,[EthicsPolicies.xlsm]Sheet1!$A$4:$B$639,2,FALSE)

2. Press Ctrl+Enter to accept the formula and keep the cell pointer in cell D2. The result will be a strange number such as 38099.

3. Press Ctrl+1 to display the Format Cells dialog. Change the numeric format to a date format.

4. Double-click the fill handle to copy the formula down to all cells.

Matching Two Lists

As shown in Figure 210, the result will show a date next to the employees who have returned their ethics statement and an #N/A next to the employees who have not.

Figure 210

Using VLOOKUP to return #N/A errors for employees who have not returned their ethics statements

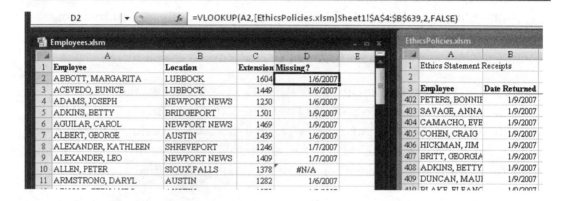

Better in Excel 2007 – Replacing #N/A

In Excel 97-2003, if you want to change the formula to show the word "Missing" instead of #N/A, you would have to actually calculate the VLOOKUP twice. The horrible formula is:

```
=IF(ISNA(VLOOKUP(A2,[EthicsPolicies.xlsm]Sheet1!$A$4:$B$639,2,FALSE)),
"Missing",VLOOKUP(A2,[EthicsPolicies.xlsm]Sheet1!$A$4:$B$639,2,FALSE))
```

Excel 2007 offers a new function called IFERROR. The function requires two arguments. The first argument is any formula that might result in an error. The second argument is the alternate value to show in case the formula is an error.

Excel calculates the formula in the first argument. If the answer is anything other than an error, the function returns the answer. Otherwise, the function returns the alternative text.

Thus, the far simpler formula in Figure 211 is:

> =IFERROR(VLOOKUP(A2,[EthicsPolicies.xlsm]Sheet1!$A$4:$B$639,2,FALSE), "Missing")

Figure 211 Excel 2007 provides many new, timesaving functions

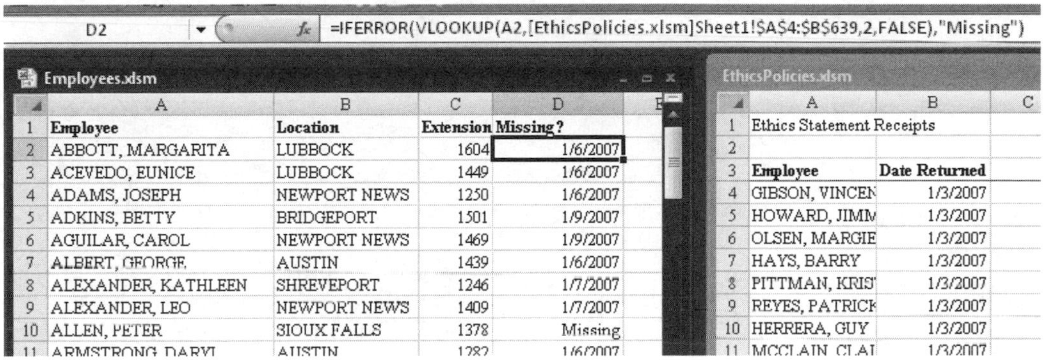

Matching Two Lists

**Matching
Two Lists**

Finding Duplicates or Unique Values

Here's the Situation

Two topics are a regular part of auditing data and are related in the methods used in Excel.

➢ As an auditor, you often want to determine if any duplicate records exist.
Did someone pay an invoice twice or double-count a bin in the inventory?

➢ You also frequently need to sift through transactional data to find a unique list of customers or vendors.

Here's What to Do

Finding Duplicates

Finding Duplicates in Excel 2007

In Excel 97-2003, you frequently would have to use the MATCH or COUNTIF functions to find if any values were duplicated.

In Excel 2007, you can quickly highlight duplicates. Follow these steps.

1. Select the range of data that might have duplicates.

2. From the Home ribbon, choose Conditional Formatting → Highlight Cell Rules → Duplicate Values…, as shown in Figure 212.

Duplicate or Unique Values

Figure 212 Select the range of customers and then apply a conditional formatting rule

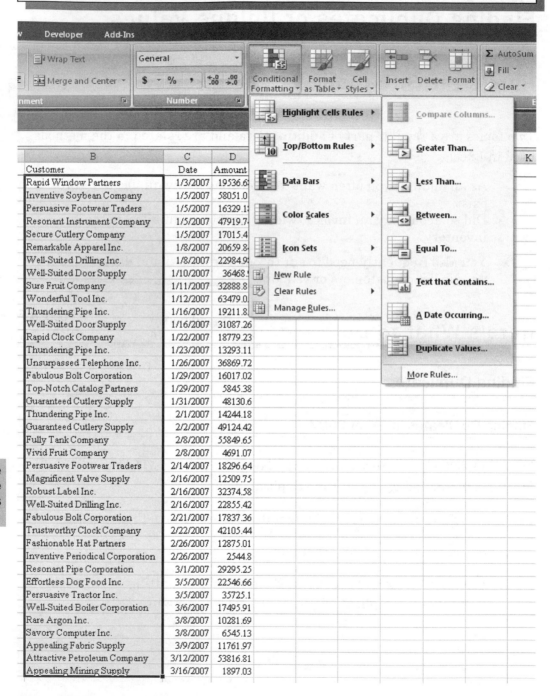

3. As shown in Figure 213, click OK in the Duplicate Values dialog.

Figure 213 Duplicates are highlighted in red

B	C	D	E	F	G	H	I
Customer	Date	Amount					
Rapid Window Partners	1/3/2007	19536.68					
Inventive Soybean Company	1/5/2007	58051.01					
Persuasive Footwear Traders	1/5/2007	16329.18					
Resonant Instrument Company	1/5/2007	47919.74					
Secure Cutlery Company	1/5/2007	17015.41					
Remarkable Apparel Inc.	1/8/200						
Well-Suited Drilling Inc.	1/8/20						
Well-Suited Door Supply	1/10/20						
Sure Fruit Company	1/11/20						
Wonderful Tool Inc.	1/12/20						
Thundering Pipe Inc.	1/16/20						
Well-Suited Door Supply	1/16/20						
Rapid Clock Company	1/22/20						
Thundering Pipe Inc.	1/23/2007	13293.11					
Unsurpassed Telephone Inc.	1/26/2007	36869.72					
Fabulous Bolt Corporation	1/29/2007	16017.02					
Top-Notch Catalog Partners	1/29/2007	5845.38					
Guaranteed Cutlery Supply	1/31/2007	48130.6					
Thundering Pipe Inc.	2/1/2007	14244.18					
Guaranteed Cutlery Supply	2/2/2007	49124.42					
Fully Tank Company	2/8/2007	55849.65					
Vivid Fruit Company	2/8/2007	4691.07					
Persuasive Footwear Traders	2/14/2007	18296.64					
Magnificent Valve Supply	2/16/2007	12509.75					
Robust Label Inc.	2/16/2007	32374.58					
Well-Suited Drilling Inc.	2/16/2007	22855.42					
Fabulous Bolt Corporation	2/21/2007	17837.36					

Duplicate Values dialog:
Format cells that contain:
Duplicate ▾ values with Red Fill with Dark Red Text ▾
OK Cancel

Duplicate or Unique Values

4. Right-click any cell in the Customer field. Choose Sort → Sort A to Z.

5. Find one cell highlighted in red. Right-click the cell and choose Sort → Put Selected Font Color On Top, as shown in Figure 214.

Figure 214 Sort by color to bring the problem cells to the top

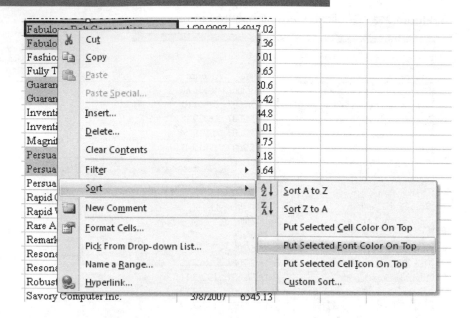

The result will be that the duplicates will be highlighted in red and appear at the top of the list as shown in Figure 215.

Figure 215

Finding duplicates in Excel 2007 is a snap

Customer	Date	Amount
Fabulous Bolt Corporation	1/29/2007	16017.02
Fabulous Bolt Corporation	2/21/2007	17837.36
Guaranteed Cutlery Supply	1/31/2007	48130.6
Guaranteed Cutlery Supply	2/2/2007	49124.42
Persuasive Footwear Traders	1/5/2007	16329.18
Persuasive Footwear Traders	2/14/2007	18296.64
Thundering Pipe Inc.	1/16/2007	19211.85
Thundering Pipe Inc.	1/23/2007	13293.11
Thundering Pipe Inc.	2/1/2007	14244.18
Well-Suited Door Supply	1/10/2007	36468.9
Well-Suited Door Supply	1/16/2007	31087.26
Well-Suited Drilling Inc.	1/8/2007	22984.98
Well-Suited Drilling Inc.	2/16/2007	22855.42
Appealing Fabric Supply	3/9/2007	11761.97
Appealing Mining Supply	3/16/2007	1897.03

Duplicate or Unique Values

Tip:

To remove the red formatting, use Home → Conditional Formatting → Clear Rules → Entire Sheet.

 Caution!

Someone at Microsoft has a twisted sense of Unique values. If you use the Duplicate Values dialog but instead ask for Unique values, then you are shown only the records that are not duplicated. As shown in Figure 216, both records of a pair of duplicates are excluded from the set. I have no idea why this would ever be useful. Later in this chapter, there will be additional examples of how to actually find the complete list of unique values.

Figure 216   Finding unique values in Excel 2007

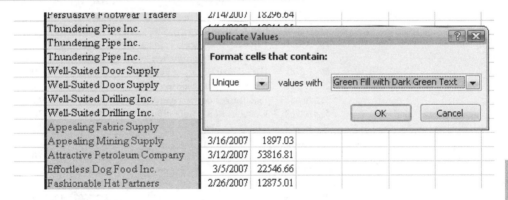

Duplicate or Unique Values

Finding Duplicates in Excel 97-2003

Finding duplicates in prior versions of Excel usually involved some fairly complex formulas.

In Figure 217, the formula in E2 will count how many times B2 occurs in column B. This formula will place a 2 next to every occurrence of duplicated records. The formula is =COUNTIF($B$2:$B$40,B2).

Figure 217

Any record with >1 in column E is part of a pair of duplicate customers

	E2			f_x	=COUNTIF($B$2:$B$40,B2)

	A	B	C	D	E
1	CustID	Customer	Date	Amount	Duplicate?
2	A8893	Wonderful Tool Inc.	1/12/2007	63479.05	1
3	A5190	Inventive Soybean Company	1/5/2007	58051.01	1
4	A4251	Fully Tank Company	2/8/2007	55849.65	1
5	A1565	Attractive Petroleum Company	3/12/2007	53816.81	1
6	A4469	Guaranteed Cutlery Supply	2/2/2007	49124.42	2
7	A4469	Guaranteed Cutlery Supply	1/31/2007	48130.6	2
8	A6653	Resonant Instrument Company	1/5/2007	47919.74	1
9	A8124	Trustworthy Clock Company	2/22/2007	42105.44	1
10	A8351	Unsurpassed Telephone Inc.	1/26/2007	36869.72	1
11	A8797	Well-Suited Door Supply	1/10/2007	36468.9	2
12	A6091	Persuasive Tractor Inc.	3/5/2007	35725.1	1
13	A7521	Sure Fruit Company	1/11/2007	32888.81	1
14	A6799	Robust Label Inc.	2/16/2007	32374.58	1
15	A8797	Well-Suited Door Supply	1/16/2007	31087.26	2
16	A6674	Resonant Pipe Corporation	3/1/2007	29295.25	1
17	A8807	Well-Suited Drilling Inc.	1/8/2007	22984.98	2
18	A8807	Well-Suited Drilling Inc.	2/16/2007	22855.42	2
19	A2841	Effortless Dog Food Inc.	3/5/2007	22546.66	1
20	A6525	Remarkable Apparel Inc.	1/8/2007	20659.84	1
21	A6258	Rapid Window Partners	1/3/2007	19536.68	1
22	A7842	Thundering Pipe Inc.	1/16/2007	19211.85	3
23	A6224	Rapid Clock Company	1/22/2007	18779.23	1
24	A6061	Persuasive Footwear Traders	2/14/2007	18296.64	2
25	A3262	Fabulous Bolt Corporation	2/21/2007	17837.36	2
26	A8787	Well-Suited Boiler Corporation	3/6/2007	17495.91	1
27	A7010	Secure Cutlery Company	1/5/2007	17015.41	1
28	A6061	Persuasive Footwear Traders	1/5/2007	16329.18	2
29	A3262	Fabulous Bolt Corporation	1/29/2007	16017.02	2
30	A7842	Thundering Pipe Inc.	2/1/2007	14244.18	3
31	A7842	Thundering Pipe Inc.	1/23/2007	13293.11	3
32	A3512	Fashionable Hat Partners	2/26/2007	12875.01	1
33	A5467	Magnificent Valve Supply	2/16/2007	12509.75	1
34	A1300	Appealing Fabric Supply	3/9/2007	11761.97	1
35	A6266	Rare Argon Inc.	3/8/2007	10281.69	1
36	A6963	Savory Computer Inc.	3/8/2007	6545.13	1
37	A7885	Top-Notch Catalog Partners	1/29/2007	5845.38	1
38	A8686	Vivid Fruit Company	2/8/2007	4691.07	1
39	A5181	Inventive Periodical Corporation	2/26/2007	2544.8	1
40	A1343	Appealing Mining Supply	3/16/2007	1897.03	1

Duplicate or Unique Values

Finding Unique Values

There are many ways to find a list of unique values in Excel. You can use a formula similar to the one in Figure 217. You can use Advanced Filter. You can use a Pivot Table. In Excel 2007, you can (carefully) use the new Remove Duplicates icon.

Using a Formula to Isolate Unique Values

The formula in Figure 218 will find only the second instance of a duplicated record. This leaves the complete set of unique records with a zero (0) in column E.

The trick here is that the range to search starts in $B$1 and extends to a relative reference to the row just above the current row. Thus, in E2, the formula is =COUNTIF($B$1:B1,B2), but in B40, the formula is =COUNTIF($B$1:B39,B40).

<table>
<tr><td rowspan="11">

Figure 218

This formula will find only the second, third, fourth, and so on occurrences of a duplicate. Anything with a zero in column E is unique.

</td><td colspan="6">E2   *fx* =COUNTIF($B$1:$B1,B2)</td></tr>
<tr><th></th><th>A</th><th>B</th><th>C</th><th>D</th><th>E</th></tr>
<tr><td>1</td><td>CustID</td><td>Customer</td><td>Date</td><td>Amount</td><td>Duplicate?</td></tr>
<tr><td>2</td><td>A8893</td><td>Wonderful Tool Inc.</td><td>1/12/2007</td><td>63479.05</td><td>0</td></tr>
<tr><td>3</td><td>A5190</td><td>Inventive Soybean Company</td><td>1/5/2007</td><td>58051.01</td><td>0</td></tr>
<tr><td>4</td><td>A4251</td><td>Fully Tank Company</td><td>2/8/2007</td><td>55849.65</td><td>0</td></tr>
<tr><td>5</td><td>A1565</td><td>Attractive Petroleum Company</td><td>3/12/2007</td><td>53816.81</td><td>0</td></tr>
<tr><td>6</td><td>A4469</td><td>Guaranteed Cutlery Supply</td><td>2/2/2007</td><td>49124.42</td><td>0</td></tr>
<tr><td>7</td><td>A4469</td><td>Guaranteed Cutlery Supply</td><td>1/31/2007</td><td>48130.6</td><td>1</td></tr>
<tr><td>8</td><td>A6653</td><td>Resonant Instrument Company</td><td>1/5/2007</td><td>47919.74</td><td>0</td></tr>
<tr><td>9</td><td>A8124</td><td>Trustworthy Clock Company</td><td>2/22/2007</td><td>42105.44</td><td>0</td></tr>
<tr><td></td><td>10</td><td>A8351</td><td>Unsurpassed Telephone Inc.</td><td>1/26/2007</td><td>36869.72</td><td>0</td></tr>
<tr><td></td><td>11</td><td>A8797</td><td>Well-Suited Door Supply</td><td>1/10/2007</td><td>36468.9</td><td>0</td></tr>
<tr><td></td><td>12</td><td>A6091</td><td>Persuasive Tractor Inc.</td><td>3/5/2007</td><td>35725.1</td><td>0</td></tr>
<tr><td></td><td>13</td><td>A7521</td><td>Sure Fruit Company</td><td>1/11/2007</td><td>32888.81</td><td>0</td></tr>
<tr><td></td><td>14</td><td>A6799</td><td>Robust Label Inc.</td><td>2/16/2007</td><td>32374.58</td><td>0</td></tr>
<tr><td></td><td>15</td><td>A8797</td><td>Well-Suited Door Supply</td><td>1/16/2007</td><td>31087.26</td><td>1</td></tr>
<tr><td></td><td>16</td><td>A6674</td><td>Resonant Pipe Corporation</td><td>3/1/2007</td><td>29295.25</td><td>0</td></tr>
<tr><td></td><td>17</td><td>A8807</td><td>Well-Suited Drilling Inc.</td><td>1/8/2007</td><td>22984.98</td><td>0</td></tr>
</table>

Duplicate or Unique Values

Sort the dataset by Column E; all of the duplicated records will be at the bottom and the unique set of customers will be at the top.

Using Advanced Filter to Find Unique Records

The Advanced Filter is capable of extracting unique records, but there are some slightly obscure steps.

Consider the Advanced Filter dialog shown in Figure 219. Although only a single cell in the original dataset was selected, Excel expanded the selection to include the entire region of data as the List Range.

Figure 219

Before invoking the Advanced Filter, build an output range with the column heading(s) corresponding to the unique values

	A	B	C	D	E	F	G	H
1	CustID	Customer	Date	Amount		Customer		
2	A8893	Wonderful Tool Inc.	1/12/2007	63479.05				
3	A5190	Inventive Soybean Company	1/5/2007	58051.01				
4	A4251	Fully Tank Company	2/8/2007	55849.65				
5	A1565	Attractive Petroleum Company	3/12/2007	53816.81				
6	A4469	Guaranteed Cutlery Supply	2/2/2007	49124.42				
7	A6653	Resonant Instrument Company	1/5/2007	47919.74				
8	A8124	Trustworthy Clock Company	2/22/2007	42105.44				
9	A8351	Unsurpassed Telephone Inc.	1/26/2007	36869.72				
10	A8797	Well-Suited Door Supply	1/10/2007	36468.9				
11	A6091	Persuasive Tractor Inc.	3/5/2007	35725.1				
12	A7521	Sure Fruit Company	1/11/2007	32888.81				
13	A6799	Robust Label Inc.	2/16/2007	32374.58				
14	A6674	Resonant Pipe Corporation	3/1/2007	29295.25				
15	A8807	Well-Suited Drilling Inc.	1/8/2007	22984.98				
16	A2841	Effortless Dog Food Inc.	3/5/2007	22546.66				
17	A6525	Remarkable Apparel Inc.	1/8/2007	20659.84				
18	A6258	Rapid Window Partners	1/3/2007	19536.68				

Advanced Filter dialog:

Action
- ○ Filter the list, in-place
- ● Copy to another location

List range: `$A$1:$D$40`
Criteria range:
Copy to: `$F$1`

☑ Unique records only

[OK] [Cancel]

To select unique values, choose the box for Unique Records Only.

Under Action, you have to select "Copy to another location" in order to enable the "Copy To" box. This is how you control which columns are considered in the unique selection.

Before invoking the Advanced Filter command, we copied the Customer heading from B1 to F1. If cell F1 is the Copy To range, then Excel will provide a unique list of customers.

If, instead, you copied Customer and Date to F1:G1, then you could specify F1:G1 as the Copy To range and get a unique list of every combination of Customer and Date.

To use Advanced Filter to get unique records, follow these steps:

1. Copy the heading(s) of the columns from which you want to extract unique values. Paste to the right of your data, leaving a blank cell as a buffer.

2. Select one cell within the dataset.

3. In Excel 97-2003: Choose Data → Filter → Advanced Filter.
    In Excel 2007: Choose Data → Sort & Filter → Advanced.

4. Click the Copy to Another Location option.

5. In the Copy To range, choose the copy of the heading(s) from Step 1.

6. Choose the box for Unique Records Only.

7. Click OK.

Excel will extract a unique list of customers. The customers will not be sorted – they will appear in the same sequence as the original data set.

Using a Pivot Table to Find Unique Records

This is the most bizarre use of pivot tables, but in Excel 97-2003, it is the absolute fastest way to create a unique set of values.

In Excel 97-2003, follow these steps:

1. Select one cell in your data.

2. Select Data → PivotTable and PivotChart Report.

Duplicate or Unique Values

3. Click Finish.

4. In the PivotTable Field List, click the Customer field and click the AddTo button. Column A will contain a unique list of customers.

5. Copy the customers and used Edit → Paste Special → Values to paste the unique list of customers.

In Excel 2007, follow these steps:

1. Select one cell in your data.

2. On the Insert ribbon, click PivotTable.

3. Click OK.

4. In the PivotTable Field List, checkmark the Customer Field. Column A will contain a unique list of customers as shown in Figure 220.

**Duplicate
or Unique
Values**

Figure 220

This is a strange, but effective use of a pivot table

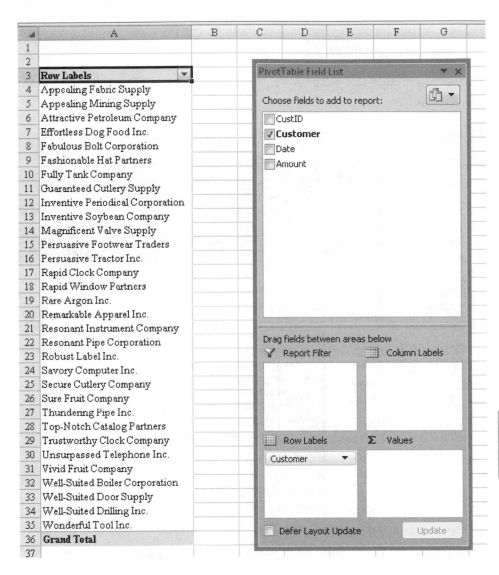

5. Copy the customers and used Edit → Paste Special → Values to paste
the unique list of customers.

Using Remove Duplicates in Excel 2007 to Find Unique Records

The new Remove Duplicates command in Excel 2007 sounds cool, but it is a very destructive command. You must use it with caution!

Before using the command, make a copy of the data. Use the Remove Duplicates command on the *copy* of the data.

In this case, copy the customer column from column B to a blank column in the worksheet.

From the Data ribbon, choose Remove Duplicates as shown in Figure 221.

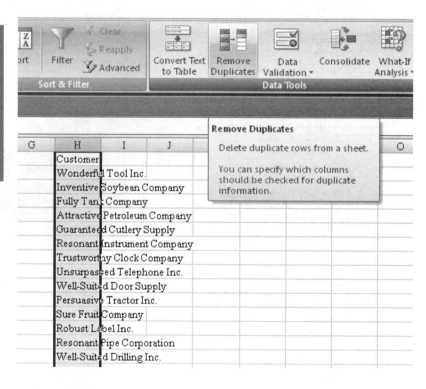

Figure 221

Be sure to make a copy of your dataset before invoking this command!

In the Remove Duplicates dialog, click OK as shown in Figure 222.

Duplicate or Unique Values

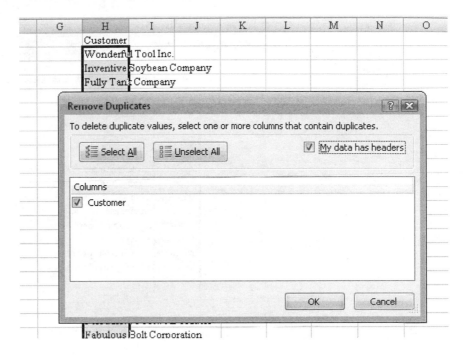

Figure 222 Remove Duplicates dialog

Excel reports on the results of the command as shown in Figure 223.

Duplicate or Unique Values

Figure 223 Duplicate values are removed from the dataset

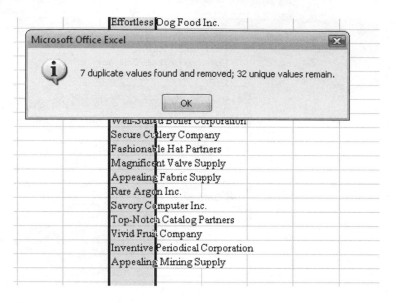

Duplicate
or Unique
Values

Finding Missing Dates in Data

Here's the Situation

You have a large dataset with a few hundred thousand records. You would like to test to see if there are any gaps in the data.

Here's What to Do

There are a couple of ways to approach this problem. One method is to sort the data, and create a new formula to test for gaps between adjacent records.

However, if your data contains dates, you will have many gaps because of weekends and holidays. You can overcome this problem by using the NETWORKDAYS function to calculate the gaps between two work days.

The other method is to use COUNTIF to count how many receipts happened on each day, as discussed in pages 121-124.

Using NETWORKDAYS

The NETWORKDAYS function is part of the Analysis ToolPack in Excel 97-2003. It has been promoted to part of the standard Excel functions in Excel 2007.

Missing Dates

If you are using Excel 2003 or earlier, you should install the Analysis ToolPack by following these steps.

1. From the menu, select Tools → Add-Ins.

2. Ensure that the Analysis ToolPack is selected.

3. Click OK.

NETWORKDAYS is a function that you might use infrequently. As a result, you might remember the function name but not the arguments. Access the Function Arguments dialog by following these steps:

1. In a blank cell, type an equals sign, the function name, and an opening parenthesis.

2. Press Ctrl+A immediately after typing the parenthesis.

3. The Function Arguments dialog box displays. Any argument names in bold are required. Other arguments are optional.

4. Click in the textbox for any argument and help for that argument displays in the lower half of the dialog, as shown in Figure 224.

Figure 224 The Function Arguments dialog provides help for each argument

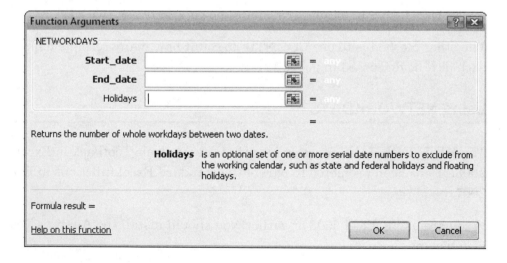

Missing Dates

At this point, you know that you will have to modify your original workbook a bit before you can enter the function. Click Cancel in the Function Arguments dialog and press Esc to exit out of the formula entry mode.

The worksheet with receipts has columns for Customer ID, Customer, Date, and Amount, as shown in Figure 225.

Figure 225

The worksheet has four columns

◢	A	B	C	D
1	XYZ Company			
2	Customer Payment Journal			
3	For the 12 months ending December 31, 2007			
4				
5	CustID	Customer	Date	Amount
363	A2059	Brilliant Carpet Inc.	1/5/2007	45843.53
364	A8133	Trustworthy Control Corporation	1/5/2007	53695.53
365	A4469	Guaranteed Cutlery Supply	1/5/2007	60827.33
366	A7717	Tasty Jet Fuel Inc.	1/5/2007	66689.42
367	A2306	Crisp Boiler Company	1/8/2007	1879.66
368	A2074	Brilliant Stamping Traders	1/8/2007	1728.1
369	A3074	Enhanced Tractor Inc.	1/8/2007	2136.92
370	A2650	Easy Argon Company	1/8/2007	1531.7
371	A5870	New Argon Inc.	1/8/2007	1835.32
372	A1925	Bright Oil Inc.	1/8/2007	1060.9

In an out-of-the-way location on the spreadsheet, type the dates for the company holidays for the date range represented by the dataset. The example dataset has dates for 2007, so Figure 226 shows the holidays for 2007 typed in range I6:I15.

Missing Dates

Figure 226

Although the cells contain dates, they are formatted as long dates to show the day of the week.

	I	J	K
1			
2			
3			
4			
5			
6	Monday, January 01, 2007		
7	Monday, May 28, 2007		
8	Wednesday, July 04, 2007		
9	Monday, September 03, 2007		
10	Monday, October 08, 2007		
11	Thursday, November 22, 2007		
12	Friday, November 23, 2007		
13	Monday, December 24, 2007		
14	Tuesday, December 25, 2007		
15	Monday, December 31, 2007		

Use the NETWORKDAYS function to compare the date in each row with the date in the previous row. If you find any gaps greater than one day, then you might find that someone accidentally deleted a range of records or something else has happened to the file.

Because you will be comparing each record to the previous record, you will want to start in your second row of data. In this example, the first formula will go in cell E7.

Follow these steps to find if there are any gaps in the dates.

1. In cell E5, enter a heading of "Delta".

2. Click on C5 and click the AZ sort button to sort by date.

3. In Cell E6, enter a value of 1.

4. In Cell, E7, type =NETWORKDAYS(
   The tooltip indicates that the first argument is the startdate.

5. Click on cell C6. Type a comma.
   The tooltip indicates that the next argument is the enddate.

6. Click on cell C7. Type a comma. The tooltip indicates that the next argument is the holidays.

Missing Dates

7. With the mouse, select I6:I15. Press the F4 key to add dollar signs to indicate that $I$6:$I$15 is an absolute reference.

8. Type the closing parenthesis.

9. The logic for NETWORKDAYS includes both the starting and ending date as 1 day. To show an actual delta, you will want to subtract 1 from the result. Type -1.

10. To accept the formula and keep the cellpointer in cell E7, press Ctrl+Enter.

11. With the cellpointer in E7, double-click the fill handle to copy the formula down to all cells.

At this point, all of the formula cells will be selected. Press Ctrl+. (that is, Ctrl+period) to move the active cell to another corner of the selection. This will show you that the last row in the range is A16306. Use the scrollbar to move a few rows down to ensure that you have captured all of the rows in the dataset.

Check the Status Bar to find the largest value in the range. If there are no gaps in the dates, you should expect a maximum value of 1.

> In Excel 97-2003: Right click the QuickSum indicator in the Status Bar and choose Max.

> In Excel 2007: Right-click the Status Bar and ensure that Max has a checkmark by it.

In Figure 227, you can see the statistics in the Status Bar. There are 16300 records. The Sum of 250 could be about right – that means, on 250 records, the date delta was 1. However, the Max indicates a problem. Somewhere in the dataset, you have a gap of eight days. Someone deleted some records from the dataset!

Missing
Dates

Figure 227 The Max delta of 8 indicates one or more problems in the dataset

	E7	▾	f_x =NETWORKDAYS(C6,C7,$I$6:$I$15)-1			
	A	B	C	D	E	F
1	XYZ Company					
2	Customer Payment Journal					
3	For the 12 months ending December 31, 2007					
4						
5	CustID	Customer	Date	Amount	Delta	
7	A7608	Sure Spring Traders	1/2/2007	1773.61	0	
8	A7429	Supreme Bottle Supply	1/2/2007	2845.66	0	
9	A6004	Persuasive Bolt Corporation	1/2/2007	3117.12	0	
10	A4823	Honest Bottle Inc.	1/2/2007	3638.5	0	
11	A5972	Paramount Machinery Company	1/2/2007	6202.29	0	
12	A8826	Wonderful Door Partners	1/2/2007	4114.09	0	
13	A4924	Ideal Curtain Corporation	1/2/2007	5009.36	0	
14	A3045	Enhanced Telephone Inc.	1/2/2007	6910.78	0	
15	A7542	Sure Fruit Supply	1/2/2007	9008.66	0	
16	A4312	Functional Valve Company	1/2/2007	14877.54	0	
17	A8390	Unsurpassed Utensil Inc.	1/2/2007	16255.87	0	
18	A7955	Top-Notch Tool Company	1/2/2007	18654.34	0	
19	A6112	Powerful Sweater Partners	1/2/2007	10519.23	0	

Receipts / Holidays

Ready | Average: 0 Count: 16300 Max: 8 Sum: 250 | 100%

Finding the Gaps

At this point, you know there is at least one gap. The next step is to find the gaps. There are several approaches.

Missing Dates

> You could use the Find command (Ctrl+F) to find cells where the value is 8. (You know the largest gap is eight days.) This approach requires you to use the Options button in the Find dialog to indicate that you want to search the values themselves instead of the formula. While this approach will find the first gap of 8, it will ignore any possible gaps of two through seven days.

> You could convert the formulas to values, and sort the data by column E descending. This would tell you how many gaps there are. You would then need to undo the sort and search for the gaps again.

> ➤ You could use the AutoFilter command to find all of the gaps > 1
> workday, as shown below. AutoFilter has been improved in Excel 2007.
> Follow the instructions below, depending on your version of Excel.

Using AutoFilter in Excel 97-2003

To flag the gaps in Excel 97-2003, follow these steps.

1. Enter a heading of "Study?" in F5.

2. Select a single cell in the dataset. For example, E5.

3. From the menu, select Data → Filter → AutoFilter. A dropdown will
    appear on each field in row 5.

4. Click the arrow to open the dropdown in E5. At the bottom of the
    dropdown is a list of all values in the column, as shown in Figure 228.
    This will show you that there is at least one gap of eight days and at
    least one gap of three days.

Figure 228

While you expected the gaps
of zero and one day, the gaps
of three and eight days point
to a problem.

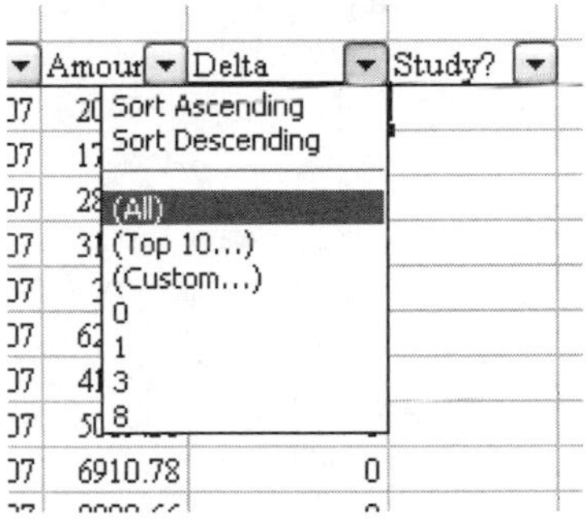

**Missing
Dates**

5. Select the 3 to display the record(s) with a gap of three days.

6. Type an "x" in column F for that record(s).

7. Repeat steps 5 and 6 to find the eight day gap(s).

8. To clear the filter, choose Data → Filter → AutoFilter. This will toggle
    off the dropdowns and show all records again.

9. From cell F5, press the End key and then the Down Arrow key in order to jump to the first gap. Continue pressing End and Down Arrow to jump to the other gaps.

Better in Excel 2007 – Using AutoFilter

To flag the gaps in Excel 2007, follow these steps.

1. Enter a heading of "Study?" in F5.

2. Select a single cell in the dataset. For example, E5.

3. On the Data ribbon, click the Filter icon. (Or, on the Home ribbon, choose Sort & Filter → Filter.) A dropdown will appear on each field in row 5.

4. Click the arrow to open the dropdown in E5. At the bottom of the dropdown are checkboxes with all values in the column, as shown in Figure 229. This will show you that there is at least one gap of eight days and at least one gap of three days.

Missing Dates

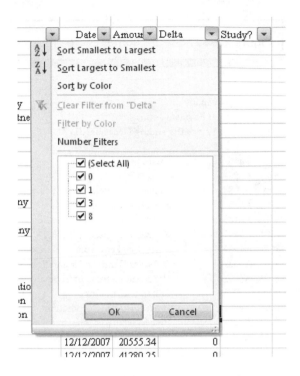

Figure 229

While you expected the gaps of zero and one day, the gaps of three and eight days point to a problem.

5. Uncheck Select All. Check the values for 3 and 8.

6. Type an "x" in column F for the visible records.

7. To clear the filter, click the Filter icon again in the Data ribbon. This will toggle off the dropdowns and show all records again.

8. From cell F5, press the End key and then the Down Arrow key in order to jump to the first gap. Continue pressing End and Down Arrow to jump to the other gaps.

Next Steps

The steps above uncovered a gap from March 16 through March 28. The 17th was a Saturday, but data is clearly missing from the 19th through the 27th – seven business days worth of receipts. This gap is shown in Figure 230. A second gap of three work days was also found in December.

Missing Dates

Figure 230 There are some records missing between rows 3709 and 3710

	A	B	C	D	E	F
1	XYZ Company					
2	Customer Payment Journal					
3	For the 12 months ending December 31, 2007					
4						
5	CustID	Customer	Date	Amount	Delta	Study?
3701	A8204	Unique Pipe Company	3/16/2007	29926.73	0	
3702	A7988	Tremendous Periodical Company	3/16/2007	54446.27	0	
3703	A7639	Swift Iron Corporation	3/16/2007	45723.15	0	
3704	A8185	Trustworthy Tool Corporation	3/16/2007	43489.63	0	
3705	A2795	Effortless Closure Company	3/16/2007	40422.52	0	
3706	A1565	Attractive Petroleum Company	3/16/2007	52537.34	0	
3707	A2539	Different Window Corporation	3/16/2007	32670.65	0	
3708	A6653	Resonant Instrument Company	3/16/2007	38766.68	0	
3709	A3049	Enhanced Tool Inc.	3/16/2007	52696.43	0	
3710	A4883	Honest Utensil Corporation	3/28/2007	17800.24	8	x
3711	A6349	Real Machinery Company	3/28/2007	16467.17	0	
3712	A3321	Fabulous Paper Company	3/28/2007	12851.95	0	

If you have found a gap, you now can do the legwork to find out what happened to the missing records. Was the entire accounts payable department closed for those days (unlikely) or did someone accidentally delete the records (likely). Go back to the source system and get the data run again.

The problem with the test in this chapter is that it would only find large gaps in the data. It doesn't indicate if someone took only a few records out.

For a way to further analyze a similar dataset, see pages 121-124.

**Missing
Dates**

Automating Excel with VBA

Here's the Situation

With 1.1 million rows in Excel, there are often times where you will need to perform repetitive tasks on each record.

Here's What to Do

Excel has a robust and powerful macro language hiding behind the cells in every copy of Excel shipped since 1995. This language can automate just about everything you can do in the Excel interface. (The only exceptions are some brand new features like inserting SmartArt diagrams in Office 2007.)

This chapter will provide some very basic short macros that you can write to automate simple tasks. It is not meant to be a comprehensive guide to VBA for Excel. If you would like to learn VBA and meet these criteria, then I would recommend that you check out *VBA & Macros for Microsoft Excel* from QUE. The criteria:

- You know the Excel interface very well

- You've tried recording a macro and it did not work

- You would like to use VBA to automate tasks in Excel

If this sounds like you, then check out the book.

Allowing VBA to Run On Your Computer

The first step to using macros is to enable VBA in your copy of Excel. In Excel 2000-2003, use Tools → Macro → Security and adjust the security to Medium. In Excel 2007, follow these steps:

1. From the Office icon menu, choose Excel Options.

2. In the Personalize category, add a checkmark next to the box for Show Developer Tab in the Ribbon.

3. In the Trust Center category, click Trust Center Options.

4. In the Macro Settings category, choose Disable All macros with Notification.

5. Close and restart Excel.

 Note:

If you are using macros in Excel 2007, you should save your workbook using the .XLSM extension.

Inserting a VBA Module in Your Workbook

A macro usually resides in a VBA Module in your workbook. Just as a workbook can contain multiple worksheets and chart sheets, a workbook can contain multiple VBA modules.

In a complex project, I might put all of the reporting macros in one module and all of the input macros in another module. Each module can contain many macros – it is up to you how you organize the macros. For the simple macros in this chapter, it is fine to put them all in one module.

To insert a module, follow these steps.

1. In Excel 97-2003: Choose Tools → Macro → Visual Basic Editor or press Alt+F11.
   In Excel 2007: Choose Developer → Visual Basic or press Alt+F11.

Automating w/ VBA

2. In the Visual Basic editor (VBE), choose Insert → Module.

Writing and Running a Macro

The large white pane on the right side of the visual basic editor is called the Code pane. You will type your macros in this pane.

To begin a macro, type the word Sub, a space, a name for the macro, and opening and closing parentheses. For example:

Sub HelloWorld()

When you type this line and press Enter, Excel creates a new macro called HelloWorld. The VBE adds a blank line and the final line of the macro with the words End Sub. Any macro commands that you type between the Sub and End Sub lines will be executed when you run the macro.

Click on the blank line between Sub & End Sub. Type a one line macro:

MsgBox "This is a test of a macro"

Figure 231 shows the VBE and your macro.

Figure 231   The Code pane is the large white area on the white side of the VBE

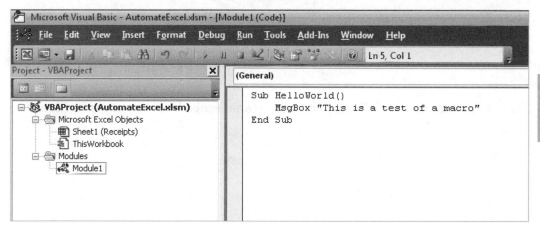

Click on the Excel icon in the Windows taskbar to return to your Excel spreadsheet. You will want to run the macro to test it.

One way to run a macro is to display the Macros dialog. This dialog can be accessed by pressing Alt+F8 in any version of Excel. In Excel 2007, you can press the Macros button on the Developer ribbon. In prior versions of Excel, use Tools → Macro → Macros.

As shown in Figure 232, The Macro dialog lists all of the macros in your workbook. (Currently, this is a single macro.) Click on a macro and press the Run button.

Figure 232

Select a macro and click Run to execute the macro

This simple macro will display the text in a message box, as shown in Figure 233.

Figure 233

Your first macro worked
successfully!

Displaying the Macro dialog is not an effective way to run a macro, particularly if you need to run the macro often. It is easier to assign the macro to a shortcut key.

Follow these steps:

1. Display the Macro dialog.

2. Click on a Macro name.

3. Choose the Options button.

4. In the Macro Options dialog, type a shortcut key for the macro as shown in Figure 234. Ctrl+J and Ctrl+K are usually safe, since there are no Excel commands assigned to those keys.

**Automating
w/ VBA**

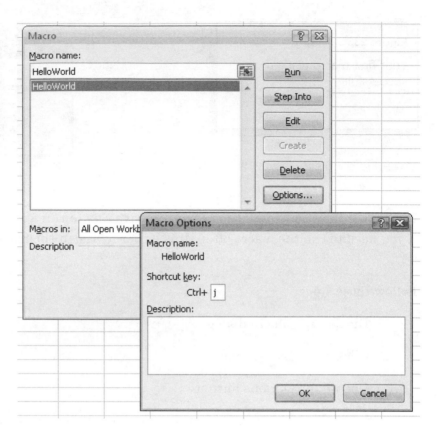

Figure 234

Assigning a shortcut key to a macro

5. Click OK to close the Macro Options dialog.

6. Click Cancel to close the Macro dialog.

You can now run the macro by just pressing Ctrl+J.

Creating a Macro to Loop Through All Records

Automating w/ VBA

A common macro follows this structure:

Start at the first data row in the worksheet.
Examine a value in one of the columns.
Based on that value, decide to *do something*.
Move to the next row in the dataset and repeat.

To create this basic macro structure, follow these steps.

1. In Excel, note the first row with data. Note the last row with data.

2. Switch to the Visual Basic Editor using Alt+F11.

3. If there is not already a module in this workbook, use Insert → Module.

4. Type the word Sub, a macro name, and (). In this example, use:
   Sub LoopSample()

5. The command for a loop is the word "For" followed by a variable name. Variables names can be I, or X, or meaningful names such as ThisRow. You need to specify the first and last rows in the loop. In the current example, the loop would be specified by:

   For ThisRow = 2 to 16171 Step 1

6. On the next line, type an apostrophe and the words "Do Something".

7. On the next line, finish the loop with the command Next ThisRow.

The simple macro in Figure 235 will loop through all of the rows of data in today's spreadsheet. The "Step 1" indicates that the macro will look at every row. If you used "Step 2", the macro would look at every other row. Right now, the only command is a comment with the note to "Do Something". The following examples will give you ideas of things the macro can do.

Figure 235

This simple loop macro will look at all of the rows in the dataset. Next, add a few lines of code to actually do something to each row.

```
(General)

Sub HelloWorld()
    MsgBox "This is a test of a macro"
End Sub

Sub LoopSample()
    For ThisRow = 2 To 16171 Step 1
        ' Do Something
    Next ThisRow
End Sub
```

Automating
w/ VBA

Referring to Cells in the Loop

You can refer to a cell at a particular row and column by using CELLS(Row,Column). For example, the cell J2 is in the second row and tenth column. CELLS(2,10) refers to cell J2.

The nice thing about the CELLS function is that either the row or column can be a variable. Thus, to refer to column D in the current row of the worksheet, use CELLS(ThisRow, 4). To refer to column A in the current row of the worksheet, use CELLS(ThisRow, 1). To refer to column E in the previous row of the worksheet, use CELLS(ThisRow − 1, 5).

Referring to an Entire Row Using CELLS

Sometimes, you might want to refer to the entire row in the loop. For example, you might want to hide the row, or color the row. Use the .EntireRow modifier. Either of these commands would hide the current row in the loop:

```
CELLS(ThisRow, 5).EntireRow.Visible = False
CELLS(ThisRow, 1).EntireRow.Visible = False
```

Referring to a Rectangular Range Using CELLS

If you were going to apply a cell color or a bold formatting, you would not want to apply it to all of the cells in the row. You might want to apply it only to the six columns actually in use in the worksheet.

The .RESIZE(# Rows, # Columns) modifier will change a CELLS command that refers to a single cell into a command that refers to a rectangular range starting from the CELL as the top left corner.

For example, to refer to a range that is one row tall and six cells wide, use

```
CELLS(ThisRow, 1).RESIZE(1, 6)
```

The following command would turn columns A:F in the current row to a red color.

```
CELLS(ThisRow, 1).RESIZE(1, 6).Interior.ColorIndex = 3
```

Macro to Color Every Third Row Red

Putting the above information together, you should be able to write a simple macro that will loop through the rows in your dataset. Change the Step command to look at every third row. Instead of the "Do Something" comment, change the color of the first six columns in that row to be red.

The macro shown in Figure 236 runs in a few seconds and is much faster than designing a new table style or a conditional format to color the rows in a white-white-red pattern.

```
Sub ColorEveryThirdRed()
    For ThisRow = 2 To 16171 Step 3
        Cells(ThisRow, 1).Resize(1, 6).Interior.ColorIndex = 3
    Next ThisRow
End Sub
```

Figure 236 The Step 3 code allows Excel to only color every third row

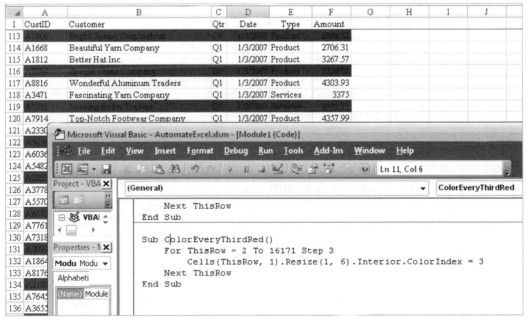

Making Decisions Based on Values in the Row

You can make decisions with the IF ... then ... Else ... End If structure. The following code would look at column E of each record. If Column E says "Services", then the value in column F is copied to column G and the row is colored green. Otherwise, the row is colored red.

```
Sub BreakOutServices()
    ' Move Service revenue from F to G
    ' Color Service rows Green
    ' Color Product rows Red
    For ThisRow = 2 To 16171 Step 1
        If Cells(ThisRow, 5) = "Services" Then
            ' Move the value from column 6 to column 7
            Cells(ThisRow, 7).Value = Cells(ThisRow, 6).Value
            ' Zero out column 6
            Cells(ThisRow, 6).Value = 0
            ' Color the row green
            Cells(ThisRow, 1).Resize(1, 7).Interior.ColorIndex = 4
        Else
            ' Put a zero in column 7
            Cells(ThisRow, 7).Value = 0
            ' Color the row red
            Cells(ThisRow, 1).Resize(1, 7).Interior.ColorIndex = 3
        End If
    Next ThisRow
End Sub
```

Automating w/ VBA

In seconds, this macro analyzes 16K+ records in Excel, rearranges the values, and applies a color as shown in Figure 237.

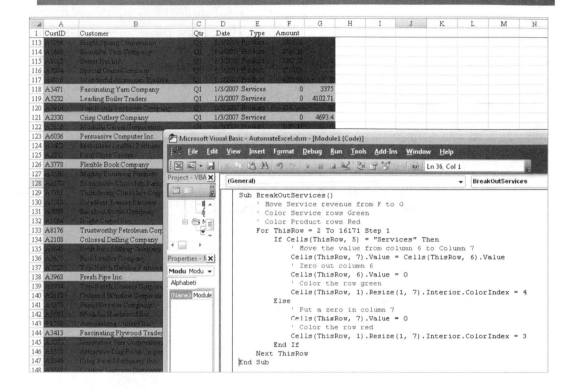

Figure 237 This basic macro loops through all rows and makes a decision based on the values in the row.

Special Handling When Deleting Rows

What if you wanted to delete the Services rows? There is a strange thing that happens in a loop when you delete a row in Excel. The row immediately below the deleted row is never tested.

Say that you have a macro that loops from row 1 to row 10.

On the fourth time through the macro, the program tests row 4 and decides to delete that row with this line of code:

```
Cells(ThisRow, 1).EntireRow.Delete
```

When you delete row 4 in Excel, all of the data in row 5 moves up to become row 4.

However, the next time through the loop, the program looks at whatever data is in Row 5. Well – this is the data that used to be in row 6.

While this sounds confusing, the important workaround is to run the loop backwards, starting at the bottom and working towards the top. You can do this by reversing the order of the rows in the FOR statement, and by specifying a step value of −1.

```
Sub DeleteQ4()
    For ThisRow = 16171 To 2 Step -1
        If Cells(ThisRow, 4) = "Q4" Then
            Cells(ThisRow, 1).EntireRow.Delete
        End If
    Next ThisRow
End Sub
```

Handling an Unknown Number of Rows

Wouldn't it be a pain to have to edit the macro every single day based on how many rows of data you have today?

There is a trick that you can use to handle a different number of rows every day. Imagine that you go to the last row of column A. Press the End key and then the Up Arrow key. Excel will jump to the final row with data in column A. You can have your macro do this. Store the resulting row in a variable with a name such as FinalRow.

Automating w/ VBA

In Excel 2003, you would use:

```
FinalRow = Cells(65536, 1).End(xlUp).Row
```

In Excel 2007, you would use:

```
FinalRow = Cells(1048576, 1).End(xlUp).Row
```

If you don't know if the program is running in Excel 2003 or Excel 2007, then you can use this slightly convoluted version:

FinalRow = Cells(Application.Rows.Count, 1).End(xlUp).Row

Working with Other Worksheets

So far, all of the macros have dealt with the active worksheet. Sometimes, you will want to move data from the active worksheet to another worksheet.

Say that you have four blank worksheets named Q1, Q2, Q3, and Q4. You want to look at each record on the active sheet and copy it to the next available row on the quarterly worksheet.

To refer to cell J2 on a sheet called Sheet3, use:

Worksheets("Sheet3").Cells(2, 10)

If your sheet name is stored in a variable called ThisQtr, then:

Worksheets(ThisQtr).Cells(2, 10)

The following macro will look at the quarter information in column D. It will assign that quarter to a variable named ThisQtr. The macro will then find the next row on the appropriate quarter worksheet and copy the record to that worksheet.

```
Sub CopyToOtherWorksheets()
    FinalRow = Cells(Application.Rows.Count, 1).End(xlUp).Row
    For ThisRow = 2 To FinalRow Step 1
        ThisQtr = Cells(ThisRow, 4)
        NextRow = Worksheets(ThisQtr).Cells(65536, 1).End(xlUp).Row + 1
        Cells(ThisRow, 1).Resize(1, 6).Copy Destination:=Worksheets(ThisQtr).Cells(NextRow, 1)
    Next ThisRow
End Sub
```

Automating
w/ VBA

Looping through all Worksheets

There is a special kind of loop known as the "For Each" loop. A workbook often contains a collection of worksheets. A worksheet contains a collection of rows. A worksheet might contain a collection of charts.

To loop through all of the objects in a collection, use:

```
For Each VariableName in Collection
  ' Do Something
Next VariableName
```

For example, to apply the red-white-white banding effect to all of the worksheets in the active workbook, you would use:

```
Sub ColorAllWorksheets()
    For Each ws In ActiveWorkbook.Worksheets
        ws.Select
        FinalRow = Cells(65536, 1).End(xlUp).Row
        For ThisRow = 2 To FinalRow Step 3
            Cells(ThisRow, 1).Resize(1, 6).Interior.ColorIndex = 3
        Next ThisRow
    Next ws
End Sub
```

Using the Macro Recorder to Learn Other Code

This book gave examples for coloring rows red or green. What if you want to turn a cell bold, pink, Tahoma, 14 point font? I don't know the code for this. You don't know the code for this. Most Excel programmers don't know the code for this. Turn on the macro recorder, format one cell, turn off the macro recorder, and examine the code.

Follow these steps to record a bit of macro code:

1. In Excel 97-2003: Use Tools → Macro → Record New Macro.
   In Excel 2007: Use Developer → Code → Record Macro.

2. The Record Macro dialog asks for a name, shortcut key, and description. You really don't care, because you will not be running this macro. Simply click OK.

3. Use formatting commands to change the current cell into bold, pink, Tahoma, 14 point font.

4. Stop the macro recorder.
    In Excel 97-2003: Press the Stop button on the tiny "Sto" toolbar.
    In Excel 2007: Click the blue stop button in the Status Bar or the Stop Recording button on the Developer ribbon.

 Note:

The "Sto" toolbar is really the "Stop Recording" toolbar, but there is not enough room on this toolbar to show the whole name.

5. Switch to the VBE with Alt+F11.

6. Excel always puts recorded code in a new module. In the Project pane, you will see there is a new Module2. Double click the module to open the code pane. You will see macro code similar to Figure 238.

Automating w/ VBA

> **Figure 238** This tiny recorded macro gives you the code for bold pink Tahoma 14 point font.

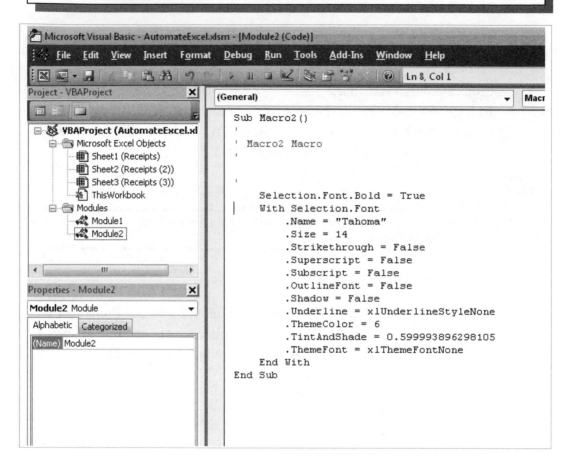

Now that you know the code from the recorded macro, you can cut and paste this section of code into your real macro back on Module 1.

The macro recorder almost always operates on the keyword Selection. In real life, macros run faster if you don't select each row. Change Selection to use the CELLS syntax, as shown below.

```
Sub ColorQ1PinkBoldTahoma()
    For ThisRow = 2 To 16171 Step 1
        If Cells(ThisRow, 4) = "Q1" Then
            Cells(ThisRow, 1).Resize(1, 6).Font.Bold = True
            With Cells(ThisRow, 1).Resize(1, 6).Font
                .Name = "Tahoma"
                .Size = 14
                .Strikethrough = False
                .Superscript = False
                .Subscript = False
                .OutlineFont = False
                .Shadow = False
                .Underline = xlUnderlineStyleNone
                .ThemeColor = 6
                .TintAndShade = 0.599993896298105
                .ThemeFont = xlThemeFontNone
            End With
        End If
    Next ThisRow
End Sub
```

A Final Note About Recording Macros

The macro recorder is really stupid.

If you record the action of moving from cell A1 to cell A2, copying A2, and pasting to B1, the macro will literally record these instructions:

> Copy A2 to B1

This macro will work if and only if the active cell is A1.

In reality, you probably wanted the macro to copy the cell below the current cell and paste it to the right of the current cell.

The macro recorder is capable of recording this code, but you have to toggle the recorder into Use Relative References mode. In Excel 2007, the icon for this is somewhat obvious, as shown in Figure 239.

Figure 239

In Excel 2007, the icon for switching into Relative Recording mode is readily discoverable.

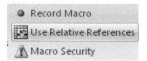

In Excel 97-2003, the icon is an obscure button on the right side of the Sto toolbar, as shown in Figure 240.

Figure 240

In previous versions of Excel, the Relative Recording icon was an unmarked obscure button on the Stop Recording Toolbar.

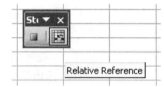

Conclusion

Thanks for using the Excel for Auditors book. I hope that we have shown you some cool tips and techniques to empower you to use the powerful features in Microsoft Excel.

If you have favorite tips to share or if you are running into a problem that is not solved in this book, drop the authors a note at auditing@MrExcel.com. We would love to hear from you in order to make the next edition of this book better.

Conclusion

Index

Index

HOLY MACRO! BOOKS QUICK ORDER FORM

Fax Orders: (707)-220-4510. Send this form.
E-Mail Orders: store@MrExcel.com – Online: http://www.MrExcel.com
Postal Orders: MrExcel, 13386 Judy Ave NW, PO Box 82, Uniontown OH 44685, USA

Quantity	Title	Price	Total
	Learn Excel from Mr Excel By Bill Jelen ISBN 1-932802-12-6 (853 pages – 2005)	$39.95	
	Excel for Teachers By Conmy, Hazlett, Jelen, Soucy ISBN 1-932802-11-8 (236 pages – 2006)	$24.95	
	Excel for Marketing Managers By Bill Jelen and Ivana Taylor ISBN 1-932802-13-4 (172 Pages – 2006)	$24.95	
	Excel for the CEO (CD-ROM) By P.K. Hari Hara Subramanian ISBN 1-932802-17-7 (351 pages – 2006)	$24.95	
	Excel for Auditors By Bill Jelen and Dwayne K. Dowel ISBN 1-932802-16-9 (212 pages – 2006)	$24.95	
	Office VBA Macros You Can Use Today By Gonzales et al ISBN 1-932802-06-1 (433 Pages – 2006)	$39.95	
	Holy Macro! It's 2,200 Excel VBA Examples (CD-ROM) By Hans Herber Bill Jelen and Tom Urtis ISBN 1-932802-08-8 (2200 pages – 2004)	$89.00	
	Slide Your Way Through Excel VBA (CD-ROM) By Dr. Gerard Verschuuren ISBN 0-9724258-6-1 (734 pages – 2003)	$99.00	
	Join the Excellers League (CD-ROM) By Dr. Gerard Verschuuren ISBN 1-932802-00-2 (1477 pages – 2004)	$99.00	
	Excel for Scientists (CD-ROM) By Dr. Gerard Verschuuren ISBN 0-9724258-8-8 (589 pages – 2004)	$75.00	
	Guerilla Data Analysis Using Microsoft Excel By Bill Jelen ISBN 0-9724258-0-2 (138 pages – 2002)	$19.95	
	The Spreadsheet at 25 By Bill Jelen ISBN 1-932802-04-5 (120 color pages – 2005)	$19.95	
	Grover Park George On Access By George Hepworth ISBN 0-9724258-9-6 (480 pages – 2004)	$29.95	
	Your Access to the World (CD-ROM) By Dr. Gerard Verschuuren ISBN 1-932802-03-7 (1450 pages – 2004)	$99.00	
	Access VBA Made Accessible (CD-ROM) By Dr. Gerard Verschuuren (1323 pages – 2004)	$99.00	
	DreamBoat On Word By Anne Troy ISBN 0-9724258-4-5 (220 pages – 2004)	$19.95	
	Kathy Jacobs On PowerPoint By Kathy Jacobs ISBN 0-9724258-6-1 (380 pages – 2004)	$29.95	
	Unleash the Power of Outlook 2003 By Steve Link ISBN 1-932802-01-0 (250 pages – 2004)	$19.95	
	Unleash the Power of OneNote By Kathy Jacobs & Bill Jelen (320 pages – 2004)	$19.95	
	VBA and Macros for Microsoft Excel By Bill Jelen and Tracy Syrstad ISBN 0789731290 (576 Pages – 2004)	$39.95	
	Pivot Table Data Crunching By Bill Jelen and Michael Alexander ISBN 0789734354 (275 Pages – 2005)	$29.95	

Name: _____
Address: _____
City, State, Zip: _____
E-Mail: _____
Sales Tax: Ohio residents add 6% sales tax
Shipping by Air: **US:** $4 for first book, $2 per additional book. $1 per CD.
                    International: $9 for first book, $5 per additional book. $2 per CD
                    FedEx available on request at actual shipping cost.
Payment: Check or Money order to "MrExcel" or pay with VISA/MC/Discover/AmEx:
               Card #:_____ Exp.:_____
               Name on Card: _____
Bulk Orders: Ordering enough for the entire staff? Save 40% when you order six or more of any one title.